D0603533

The Illustrated Book of Patriotism

The History of Britain and The World

By
George Courtauld

'This story shall the good man teach his son'
For my boys with all my love

EBURY PRESS

St George, the patron saint of England, in the stained glass window at the RAF Memorial chapel, Biggin Hill, Kent.

The following photographs and illustrations are reproduced by kind permission of E&E Picture Library: p.5, p.7, p.8–13, p.15–23, p.27–38, p.40–48, p.50, p.51, p.53, p.55, p.58, p.60, p.62, p.65, p.68–72, p.80. p.84, p.86, p.89, p.90, p.91, p.98, p.102, p.105, p.106, p.109, p.110, p.111, p.112, p.114, p.115, p.121, p.123, p.124, p.134–140, p.143. The publishers are grateful to the following photographers for the use of their work: Stapleton Collection, D. Burrows, S. Waterson, D. Anson, B. Andrews, R. Pilgrim, E. Osaki Owen, D. Fusaro, S. Coyne, Martin Hall, E. Disney, R. Fox, K. Murrell, N. Board, C. Millington, P. Mott, D. Toase. Every effort has been made to contact and clear permissions with relevant copyright holders. In the event of any omissions please contact the Publishers with any queries.

First published in Great Britain by Ebury Publishing in 2006

1 3 5 7 9 10 8 6 4 2

Ebury Publishing
Random House, 20 Vauxhall Bridge Road, London SW1V 2SA

Random House Australia (Pty) Limited
20 Alfred Street, Milsons Point, Sydney, New South Wales 2061, Australia

Random House New Zealand Limited
18 Poland Road, Glenfield, Auckland 10, New Zealand

Random House South Africa (Pty) Limited
Isle of Houghton, Corner Boundary Road & Carse O'Gowrie, Houghton, 2198, South Africa

Random House Publishers India Private Limited
301 World Trade Tower, Hotel Intercontinental Grand Complex, Barakhamba Lane, New Delhi 110 001, India

The Random House Group Limited Reg. No. 954009
www.randomhouse.co.uk
A CIP catalogue record for this book is available from the British Library.

Designer: David Fordham
Picture Researchers: Isobel Sinden and Vanessa Fletcher

The publishers would like to thank the following for their kind permission to reproduce illustrations: p.6 Atlas of Canada/NRC; p.103 NARA; p.120 Library of Congress; p.125 NARA; p.125 US Airforce; p.129 NASA; p.132 US Airforce.

ISBN: 0091909678
ISBN-13 [from January 2007]: 9780091909673
Papers used by Ebury Press are natural, recyclable products made from wood grown in sustainable forests.

Printed and bound by C&C Offset Printing Co., Ltd

Contents

Introduction

Other than getting married and having children, publishing *The Pocket Book of Patriotism* has been the greatest and most gratifying adventure of my life. Having put together a history chart for my three boys over the Christmas holidays, I pinned it on the bathroom wall and assumed that was that. It was no more than a simple timeline with 'Britain' on the left and 'Abroad' on the right; beginning with Stonehenge and the Great Pyramid of Khufu, and ending with the Rugby World Cup; peppered with those magnificent British quotes that still make our hair stand on end and bring tears to our eyes.

But almost from day one, the chart took on a life of its own. Within a matter of weeks we were bombarded with requests for photocopies. Both in our early forties, my wife is a nurse, working locally as an NHS health visitor, and I commute up to London to work as a head-hunter. Neither of us are scholars. The timeline was just one ordinary father's take on British history, triggered by a casual piece of eavesdropping on the train. Going home on Christmas Eve I had overheard six happy, engaging children admit their confusion over who Nelson was.

Anxious that my own sons not be similarly deprived I dragooned them into helping make the chart. Not for one moment did we think it might ever be published. But when people who had seen copies of copies started ringing asking for copies, it occurred to me that publishing was precisely what we ought to do.

Perhaps because of the narrow modern focus on certain periods at school and the current compulsion to airbrush away great swathes of our past, coupled with a fashionable insistence on 'equivalence' (that everything is pretty much the same and that, accordingly, nothing is in any way special), an entire generation of parents in Britain is now anxious. Anxious that not only do their children have no idea of the simple order in which things happened, but that they also have no concept of what a wonderful country this is – how gallant, generous and dogged, exceptional, eccentric and blessed – how special.

It seemed there was an aching thirst for something, an outline of British history without judgement, padding or fashionable distortion, setting out the milestones (whether you approve of them or not), to help us pass on our heritage.

Over the next few months I went over it again, checking, editing and expanding. Gradually it evolved into a book. It was time to pick a name. The ancient Greeks described barbarians as people who have no memory. It seems to me, however, that what we choose to remember, what we select to guide and inspire us, dictates more than just our memory, it shapes our very identity; our national character. I decided to call it *The Pocket Book of Patriotism*.

Henry VIII's older brother Arthur, Prince of Wales, who died in 1502 and whose widow, Catherine of Aragon, Henry married.

I managed to persuade seven publishing houses to meet me, but all rejected the project out of hand. They felt the use of the word 'patriotism' in the title was at best distasteful, if not downright offensive. I was even assured that patriotism was an obsolete concept. I resolved to publish it myself.

On Thursday, November 18, 2004, the first 10,000 books rolled off the presses – and it took off. We were deluged with faxes, emails, letters and telephone calls. Order piled upon order to the extent that we used up the entire stock of cream British paper in the country. In less than a month we had shipped 140,000 books.

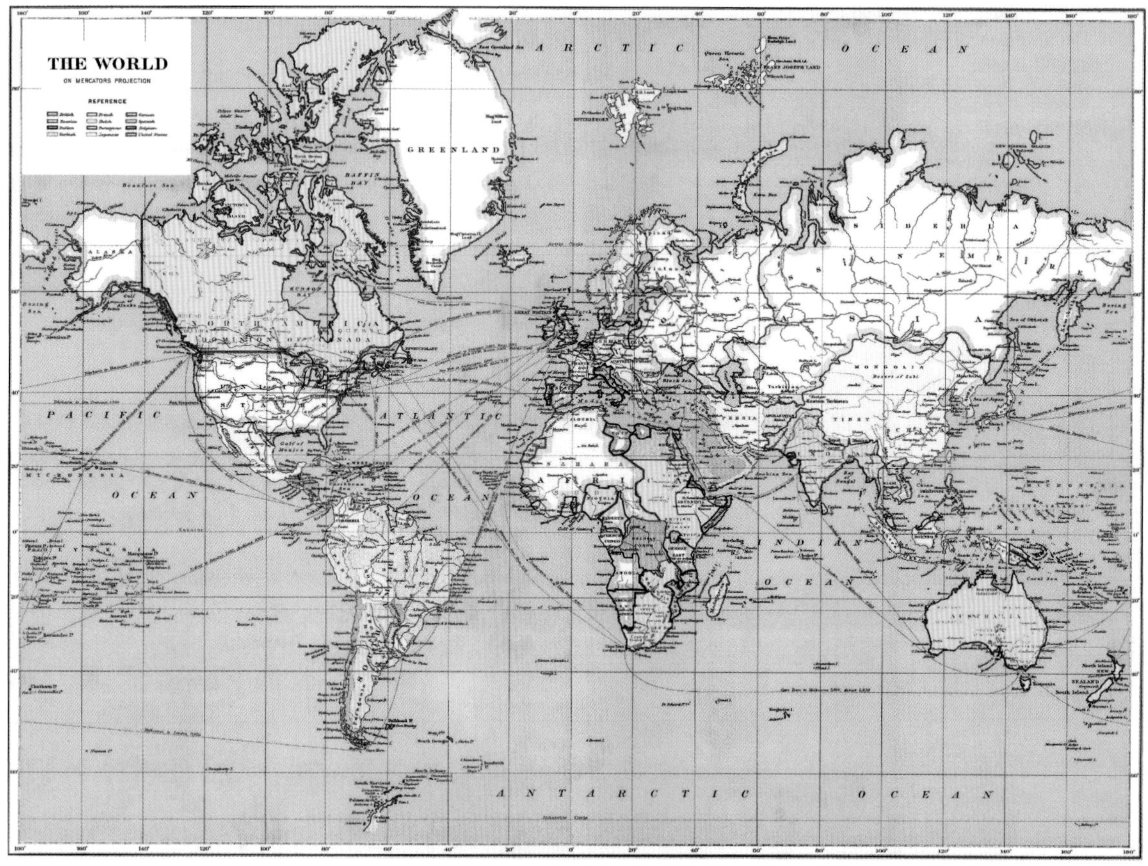

The British Empire in 1914, with its territories outlined in pink, evolved into the Commonwealth, described by the Queen in 1953 as built on 'friendship, loyalty and the desire for freedom and peace'.

What took our breath away was the great wall of goodwill that descended upon us. Thousands and thousands wrote wishing us well. People from all religions, races and walks of life, keen to share their love of Britain, their pride in our past and present, to nominate their favourite quotes, point out omissions, suggest additions and recommend illustrations, all felt compelled to get in touch.

Many bought the book to share with children, something they said would be hugely enhanced by pictures. So here it is, *The Illustrated Book of Patriotism*, expanded and I hope improved, many of the new entries suggested by readers.

I still can't believe that our scruffy homemade poster has, with the help of Ebury Press, somehow evolved into this beautiful book. If researching our glorious national story over the past two years has taught me anything, it is that we ARE special. I hope this helps illustrate why.

The History of Britain and The World

2550 TO 800 BC

A Victorian illustration of Stonehenge as it might have looked when still in tact.

BRITAIN

2200–1300 BC ~ Stonehenge

c. **1000 BC** ~ The first hill-forts

800 BC ~ The Celts arrive in Britain

Ancient Greek geographers describe the 'Keltoi' as a barbarian people from the Alpine regions of present-day Southern Europe, Spain and Portugal. They arrived in Britain in a series of waves over several centuries; they also reached modern-day Turkey, Italy and Germany.

ABROAD

c. **2550 BC** ~ The Great Pyramid of Khufu

c. **1900–1500 BC** ~ The Hindu Vidas compiled

c. **1750 BC** ~ The Babylonian eye-for-an-eye law

c. **1250 BC** ~ The Trojan War

c. **1225 BC** ~ Moses given the Ten Commandments

970 BC ~ The death of King Solomon of Israel

c. **900 BC** ~ Homer's *Iliad* and *Odyssey*

776 BC ~ The first Olympic Games held in Athens
753 BC ~ Rome founded by Romulus and Remus

c. **604–531 BC** ~ The life of Lao-tzu, founder of Taoism

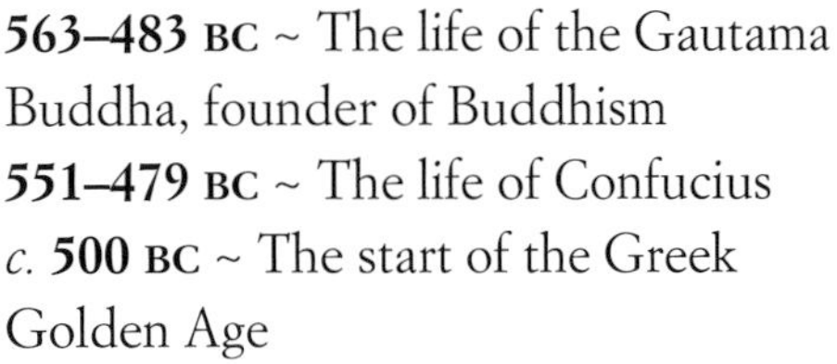

563–483 BC ~ The life of the Gautama Buddha, founder of Buddhism
551–479 BC ~ The life of Confucius
c. **500 BC** ~ The start of the Greek Golden Age

490 BC ~ Greek victory over the Persians at the Battle of Marathon
c. **480 BC** ~ The Greek fleet defeats Xerxes's Persians at the Battle of Salamis

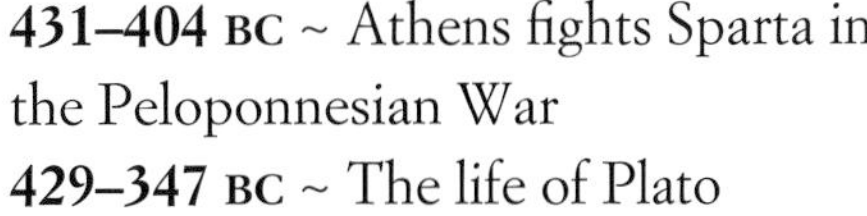

431–404 BC ~ Athens fights Sparta in the Peloponnesian War
429–347 BC ~ The life of Plato

399 BC ~ The trial and death of Socrates
384–332 BC ~ The life of Aristotle

356–323 BC ~ The life of Alexander the Great

Buddha, from the sanscrit 'The Enlightened'.

264–146 BC ~ The Punic Wars fought between Rome and Carthage
218 BC ~ The Carthaginian general Hannibal leads his army over the Alps
214 BC ~ The Great Wall of China completed
206 BC–AD 220 ~ The Han dynasty, China

55 TO 3 BC

55 BC ~ Julius Caesar's first invasion of Britain

Interested in Britain as an essential source of minerals, especially tin, Caesar was also enraged by the Britons' support of the Gauls in modern-day France, and eager for further military triumphs. Through a combination of the weather, guerrilla tactics and his own quest for personal power back in Rome, Caesar eventually lost interest.

54 BC ~ Julius Caesar's second invasion of Britain

Returning to Britain with four legions, Caesar forced the British tribes to formally submit and pay tribute, after which he withdrew.

44 BC ~ Julius Caesar assassinated

27 BC–AD 14 ~ Octavian Augustus becomes the first Emperor of Rome

3 BC ~ The Birth of Jesus

'I am the way, the truth and the life.'
Jesus

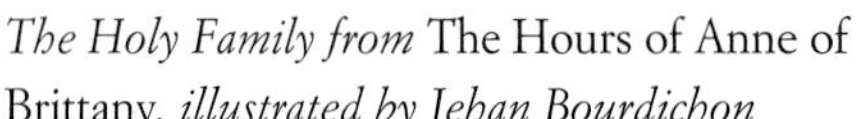

The Holy Family from The Hours of Anne of Brittany, *illustrated by Jehan Bourdichon*

The Crucifixion, showing the spear with which Longinus wounded the crucified Jesus, which, according to legend, Joseph of Arimathea brought to Britain with the Holy Grail in the year 63.

AD **30** ~ Jesus crucified

AD **43** ~ The Roman invasion and conquest of Britain

The Roman Emperor Claudius, anxious to consolidate his rule with a great military victory, sent an army of 40,000 men, plus elephants, to subdue Britain. Once victory was assured, Claudius travelled to Britain to accept in person the surrender of the British tribes. He remained on British soil for 15 days.

47 ~ The Fosse Way completed

50 ~ London founded

60 ~ The Druids smashed by the Romans on Anglesey

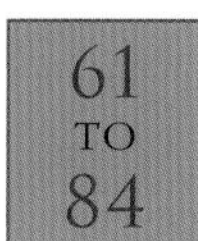

61 TO 84

1st Century

61 ~ Boadicea leads the Iceni in revolt against the Romans:

Boadicea, or Boudicca, meaning Victory, in her scythed war chariot.

'I fight not for my kingdom or for booty, but for my love of freedom, my bruised body, my outraged daughters. We will win this battle or perish! This is what I a woman will do! Men may live in slavery!'

64 ~ Rome burnt and Christians persecuted under Emperor Nero

70–84 ~ The Romans conquer Wales and the North

77–84 ~ Agricola Roman Governor

84 ~ The Battle of Mons Graupius, the Romans defeat the Caledonians:

70 ~ The Romans sack Jerusalem and destroy the Temple

79 ~ The eruption of Mt Vesuvius destroys the city of Pompeii

80 ~ The Colosseum of Rome completed

'To plunder, butcher, steal, these things they misname Empire: They make a desolation and they call it peace.'

CALGACUS, CHIEF OF THE CALEDONIANS. FROM TACITUS

105 ~ Paper invented in China

122 ~ Work starts on Hadrian's wall

Named after the Emperor Hadrian, the wall, running between the River Tyne and the Solway Firth, was designed to keep the Scottish tribes at bay, but there was always trouble beyond it. In 145 the Antonine Wall was constructed further north, and in 210 the Emperor Septimus Severus personally launched a punitive campaign as far north as Aberdeen. He died at York in 211, the only Roman Emperor to be buried on British soil.

c. **300** ~ The stirrup invented

The head of Constantine the Great on a contemporary coin.

304 ~ The death of St Alban, the first Christian to be martyred in Britain

306 ~ Constantine the Great declared Roman Emperor at York

304 ~ The Martyrdom of St George

313 ~ The Edict of Milan, grants official tolerance to Christianity in the Roman Empire

330 ~ Constantine the Great founds Constantinople

367 ~ Saxons arrive on the Saxo Shore

The Saxons came from Northern Germany, armed with the sea axe, a short sword ideal for fighting on ship. The term 'Anglo-Saxon' covers all the peoples invading Britain from Germany and Denmark, at this time, including the Angles and Jutes. Their concepts of civic responsibility, the function of Law and the obligation of the Crown to listen to recognized advisers still influences Britain today.

395 ~ The Roman Empire splits into East and West

397 ~ *The Confessions* of St Augustine

400 TO 450

5th Century

409 ~ The Roman legions abandon Britain

By 400 Rome was in terminal decline, under threat from the Visigoths and other barbarians. Outlying legions were gradually recalled for Rome's own defence, and the Provinces had to fend for themselves.

c. **446** ~ The British make their final plea for help from Rome:

400 ~ The British monk Pelagius denies the importance of Original Sin

410 ~ Rome sacked by the Visigoths

'To Aetius, thrice consul, the groans of the Britons. The barbarians push us to the sea, the sea pushes us back on the barbarians. Between these two kinds of death we are either drowned or slaughtered.'

450–750 ~ Britain is settled by the Angles, Saxons and Jutes, gradually evolving into the Seven Kingdoms of Northumbria, Mercia, East Anglia, Wessex, Essex, Sussex and Kent

St Columba, whose name means dove, and who used Iona as a missionary stepping stone for Scotland and the Isles.

BRITAIN ❋ ABROAD

450 ~ Kent is settled by the Saxons Hengist and Horsa

In return for military services against the invading Picts, the Saxons were offered money and temporary settlement in Kent by the British High King or Vortigern.

453 ~ The death of Attila the Hun

455 ~ The Saxon Hengist turns on the British Vortigern

460 ~ St Patrick returns to convert Ireland:

455 ~ Rome sacked by the Vandals

'Today I put on a terrible strength, invoking the trinity, confessing the three with faith in the one as I face my maker.'

469 ~ The Visigoths invade Spain

476 ~ The last Roman Emperor of the West overthrown

510 ~ The Battle of Mount Badon, the Britons defeat the Saxons

529 ~ The Benedictine order founded by St Benedict

534 ~ The Justinian law code

537 ~ The Haghia Sophia of Constantinople completed

563–7 ~ St Columba established on Iona:

'Christ is my druid.'

570–80 ~ The Anglo-Saxons consolidate their hold on the British lowlands

'Not Angles, but Angels.'

POPE GREGORY ON SEEING ANGLE SLAVES

6th ~ 7th Century

597 ~ St Augustine reaches Britain renewing contact with Rome

After the Romans abandoned Britain in the 5th century, the original Romano-British Christians lost touch with Rome. The spiritual descendants of St Patrick spread their own brand of Celtic Christianity with an emphasis on monasteries. The Celtic Christians and the Romano-British Christians were understandably wary of the Pagan Saxons who dominated the British lowlands: an opportunity for the Roman Church of Augustine to convert them.

St Augustine with the Scallop shell of a pilgrim resting on a bible. He was sent to Britain by Pope Gregory who so admired the Angle slaves.

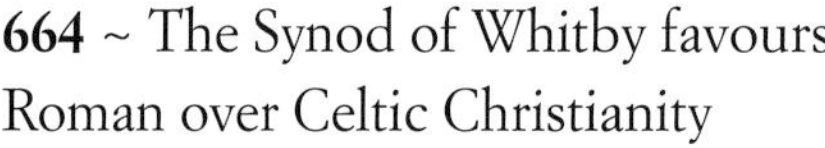

664 ~ The Synod of Whitby favours Roman over Celtic Christianity

Oswy, King of Northumberland and a Celtic Christian, called the Synod of Whitby to remedy the fact that he was celebrating Easter while his wife, a member of the Roman Church, was still keeping her Lent fast. Hilda, the Abbess of Whitby, supervised the Synod which opted for Roman rule.

673–735 ~ The life of the Venerable Bede, the 'Father of English History'

698 ~ The *Lindisfarne Gospels*

619–906 ~ The Tang Dynasty, China
625 ~ Mohammed starts reciting the Koran

674–8 ~ The Arabs besiege Constantinople

8th Century

711 ~ The Arabs reach Spain

732–3 ~ The Moors (Muslims) defeated by the Frankish leader Charles Martel at the Battle of Tours

750 ~ *Beowulf*

751 ~ The Buddhist *Diamond Sutra*, the first printed book

757–96 ~ King Offa rules Saxon Mercia

788 ~ Work starts on the Great Mosque at Córdoba, Spain

789 ~ Offa's Dyke constructed

Christianity did not bring peace to the British Isles. The Kings fought amongst themselves. King Offa of Mercia ruled a kingdom south of the River Humber. He built a 160-mile earthwork from the mouth of the Wye to the mouth of the Dee to protect his Kingdom. It was 6ft deep with a 25ft rampart.

The interior of the dome of The Great Mosque at Córdoba.

793 ~ Viking raids begin

The life of the Vikings, Norsemen, or Danes, who came from Denmark, Sweden and Norway, was intimately bound up with war-making, or *Viking*, and with the sea, which they called 'the silver necklace of the earth'. The sea-faring Vikings perfected clinker-built longships and navigated by the stars, calculating latitude from the shadow of a notched stick. Their long boats reached India, Russia and America. Contemptuous of Christianity, they came in search of booty, slaves and land.

'Behold the church of St Cuthbert, spattered with the blood of the priests of God.'

Alcuin of York, Charlemagne's Court Scholar, on hearing of the sack of Lindisfarne

Britain | Abroad

9th Century

800 ~ The *Book of Kells*

800 ~ Charlemagne of France crowned Holy Roman Emperor

866 –77 ~ Invasion of the Great Danish (or Viking) Army

867 ~ The Danes take Northumbria and march down to East Anglia

869 ~ (St) Edmund, King of East Anglia, dies fighting the Danes

A wall painting of St Edmund in St Mary's church, Boxford.

870 ~ Gunpowder invented in China

871 ~ The Battle of Ashdown: the West Saxons, led by Alfred of Wessex, defeat the Danes

THE REIGN OF ALFRED THE GREAT, KING OF WESSEX (871–99)

Saxon scholar and warrior king around whom a unified country eventually evolved

886 ~ The North subjected to the Danelaw, the rule of the Danes

889 ~ The *Anglo-Saxon Chronicle* begun

889 ~ Angkor founded as capital of the Khmer Empire in modern-day Cambodia

890 ~ Alfred translates Gregory's *Pastoral Care*:

'Our ancestors, who formally held these places, loved wisdom, and through it they obtained wealth and left it to us. Here we can still see their footprints but we cannot track after them…Therefore it seems better to me that we translate certain books into the language we can all understand.'

King Alfred holding a scroll in Cheshire All Saints Church, Siddington. The only English monarch accorded the title 'Great'.

THE REIGN OF EDWARD THE ELDER, ELDEST SON OF ALFRED THE GREAT (899–924)

910–19 ~ Edward conquers much of the Danelaw

920 ~ Northumbria subdued

910 ~ The Benedictine Abbey at Cluny founded

911 ~ Rollo the Viking hailed as the first Duke of Normandy

10th Century

THE REIGN OF ATHELSTAN, REX TOTIUS BRITANNIAE,
King of all Britain
(924–39)

'Athelstan the King, of Earls the Lord, rewarder of heroes.'

Britain	Abroad
927 ~ Athelstan invades Northumbria, subduing the monarchs of Strathclyde and Scotland	**933** ~ Delhi founded
937 ~ The Battle of Brunanburgh, Athelstan crushes the combined force of Scottish, Irish and Viking kings, becoming overlord of Celtic kingdoms in Cornwall, Scotland and Wales	

THE REIGN OF EDMUND THE ELDER,
The Deed-Doer
(939–46)

942–4 ~ Edmund retrieves the Five Danish Boroughs from Viking overlords, and recaptures parts of the Midlands and Northumbria, seized by the Irish after Athelstan's death

945 ~ Strathclyde subdued

946 ~ Viking York and Northumbria regained

THE REIGN OF EDRED
(946–55)

947 ~ Northumbria raided by Irish Norsemen and Eric Bloodaxe of York

954 ~ Edred finally secures Northumbria and expels Bloodaxe

THE REIGN OF EDWIG THE FAIR
(955–9)

955 ~ Dunstan, Abbot of Glastonbury, expelled from court

957 ~ Mercia and Northumbria reject Edwig in favour of his younger brother, Edgar

THE REIGN OF EDGAR THE PEACEFUL
(959–75)

'Edgar the Glorious, by the Grace of Christ illustrious King of the English.'

961–88 ~ Dunstan reinstated as chief advisor and Archbishop of Canterbury

962 ~ Otto I crowned Holy Roman Emperor

973 ~ The British princes acknowledge Edgar as their overlord

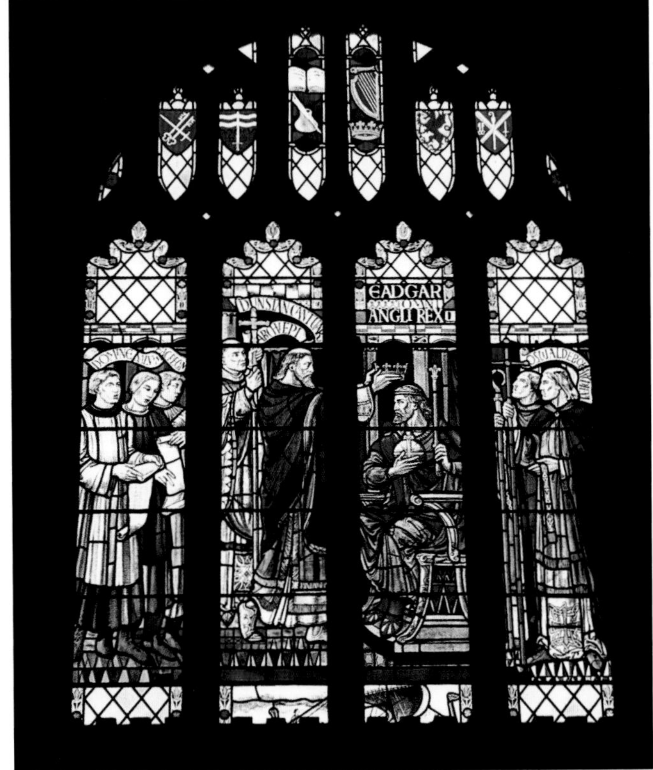

Stained glass window in Wells Cathedral showing the coronation of King Edgar in Bath.

THE REIGN OF EDWARD THE MARTYR
(975–8)

978 ~ The young king's brief reign ends in his murder, elevating him to a symbol of wronged innocence. Miracles at his tomb lead to his canonization in 1002

THE REIGN OF ETHELRED THE UNREADY
(978–1016)

980 ~ Danish (or Viking) invasions resumed

987 ~ Hugh Capet crowned King of France

991 ~ The Battle of Maldon, Vikings defeat the Saxons

991 ~ Ethelred buys off the Vikings with Danegeld

992 ~ Venice and Byzantium make their first formal trading agreement

1002 ~ Ethelred marries Emma of Normandy

1002 ~ Ethelred massacres Danish settlers, provoking invasion by the Danish King Sweyn

1013 ~ Fleeing to Normandy, Ethelred returns after Sweyn's death in 1014

Brass of Ethelred the Unready in Wimbourne Minster, Dorset. He seems not only to have been badly advised but vicious and inept.

11th Century

THE REIGN OF EDMUND IRONSIDE, SON OF ETHELRED (1016)

1015–16 ~ Resisting the Viking occupation of England by Canute the Dane, son of Sweyn, Edmund brilliantly regains control of the South and accepts the submission of the five Danish boroughs

1016 ~ The Battle of Ashington, Edmund and his Saxons are defeated by the Danes and forced to share England with Canute

THE REIGN OF CANUTE THE DANE (1016–35)

After Edmund's death the Saxon Witan accepts Canute as King, England being incorporated into his Scandinavian empire. Canute conciliated the English, however, by marrying Ethelred's widow, Emma of Normandy, and converting to Christianity.

1019 ~ Canute becomes King of Denmark

1027–8 ~ The king makes a pilgrimage to Rome

1028 ~ Canute conquers Norway

1031 ~ Homage received from Scotland

1035 ~ William, the future Conqueror of England, proclaimed Duke of Normandy

THE REIGN OF HAROLD I, HAROLD HAREFOOT (1035–40)

On Canute's death, his sons, Harthacanute and Harold, share the kingdom, with Harold acting as Regent while his half-brother fights to retain his Danish throne.

1037 ~ In Harthacanute's absence, Harold has himself proclaimed King of England

1040 TO 1065

11th Century

THE REIGN OF HARTHACANUTE,
KING OF DENMARK AND ENGLAND
(1040–2)

1040 ~ On Harold's death, Harthacanute returns to reclaim the English throne before his sudden death two years later

1041–8 ~ Movable type invented in China by Pi Sheng

THE REIGN OF EDWARD THE CONFESSOR
(1042–66)

Edward, the pious son of Ethelred the Unready and Emma of Normandy, restores the Saxon line of Wessex.

1047 ~ Harold Hardrada, King of Norway, makes peace with England

1051–2 ~ Edward banishes his father-in-law, Godwin, Earl of Wessex, and antagonizes English nobles by placing Normans in positions of power

1053 ~ Godwin's son, Harold Godwinson, inherits the old Earl's lands and influence

1054 ~ The Great Schism, the Church splits into the Roman Church of the West and the Orthodox Church of the East

1055 ~ Seljuk Turks reach Baghdad

1063 ~ Harold Godwinson, fighting in Wales

1065 ~ Westminster Abbey consecrated

THE REIGN OF HAROLD II
(1066)

When Edward the Confessor died childless, three rivals competed for the English throne: Harold Hardrada, the King of Norway, William the Bastard, the Duke of Normandy (the future Conqueror) and Harold Godwinson, Earl of East Anglia, Wessex and Kent, brother to Queen Edith, Edward the Confessor's wife. As Harold of Wessex was the only claimant actually in the country at Edward's death, he immediately had himself crowned and marched north with lightening speed to confront the giant Harold Hardrada.

'I will give him seven feet of English ground, or as much more as he may be taller than other men!'

HAROLD'S REPLY TO THE GIANT HARDRADA'S DEMAND FOR ENGLAND.

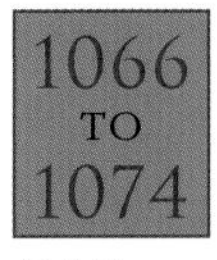

11th Century

1066 ~ The Battle of Stamford Bridge, the Saxons, led by the new King Harold, crush the invading Vikings under Harold Hardrada

1066 ~ The Battle of Hastings, the invading Normans, led by William, defeat the exhausted Saxons under Harold, who dies on the field:

'By the Splendour of God I have taken possession of my realm; the earth of England is in my two hands.'

WILLIAM OF NORMANDY, AFTER TRIPPING ON LANDING AT PEVENSEY AND RISING TO HIS FEET WITH SAND IN HIS HANDS.

A section of The Bayeux Tapestry in which the Normans learn of Harold's approach.

THE HOUSE OF NORMANDY

THE REIGN OF WILLIAM I, THE CONQUEROR (1066–87)

Descended from Vikings, or Norsemen, the Normans settled in France and established the Viking Duchy of Normandy *c.* 911.

1069 ~ The Harrying of the North. The Conqueror lays waste to the North

1070 ~ Work starts on Canterbury Cathedral

1071 ~ Hereward the Wake and other rebels resist the Conqueror's rule from the Isle of Ely

1071 ~ Seljuk Turks take Jerusalem

1074 ~ The Bayeux tapestry

BRITAIN | ABROAD

1078 TO 1100

11th ~ 12th Century

1078 ~ Work starts on the Tower of London

1085 ~ The Moors ejected from Toledo, Spain

1086–7 ~ *The Domesday Book:*

'There was no single hide nor indeed was one ox, one cow or one pig...not put down in his record.'

THE REIGN OF WILLIAM II, RUFUS THE REDHEAD (1087–1100)

1088 ~ Rebellious Barons, supporting Rufus's elder brother Robert, Duke of Normandy, subdued

1091–4 ~ William invades Normandy
1093 ~ King Malcolm III of Scotland killed by the English at Alnwick
1093–7 ~ Anselm Archbishop of Canterbury:

'Why did God become Man? Because it was necessary.'

1094 ~ El Cid takes Valencia from the Moors
1096–9 ~ The First Crusade, the Christians retake Jerusalem

1097–8 ~ Fighting in Wales
1100 ~ The king shot down hunting in the New Forest

1100 ~ The Ceremony of Marriage to the Sea first performed in Venice

THE REIGN OF HENRY I, BEAUCLERC (1100–35)

'An illiterate King is a crowned ass.'

1100–9 ~ Anselm returns as Archbishop of Canterbury, promoting the doctrine that the Pope should take precedence over all earthly rulers
c. **1100–35** ~ The Curia Regis, the forerunner of Parliament, assumes a greater role

12th Century

1106 ~ Henry invades and seizes Normandy at the Battle of Tinchebrai, imprisoning his elder brother Robert in Cardiff Castle

The Templar seal of Two Knights on horseback in the Temple Church, London – the first master being so poor he had to share a horse.

1120 ~ The Wreck of the *White Ship*. Henry loses his only son and heir, William the Atheling (so named because of his Saxon mother), who drowns at sea, dashing all the king's hopes. Henry is reputed never to have smiled again

1128 ~ Cistercian Monks arrive in Britain

The Cistercians' particularly harsh interpretation of the Benedictine rule led them to use undyed wool for their habits, giving rise to their nickname, the 'white monks'. The Cistercians admitted laybrothers for manual labour, and provided rest for travellers, as well as schools, hospitals and libraries. Many abbeys became enormously rich.

1116 ~ Bologna University founded
1118 ~ The Knights Templar established

Knights Templar being blessed in St Botolph's Church, Lincolnshire. They swore to protect pilgrims travelling to the Holy Places.

1131 TO 1147

12th Century

1131 ~ The Abbeys of Tintern, Rievaulx and Fountains founded

THE REIGN OF STEPHEN
Contesting Control with His Cousin the Empress Matilda
(1135–54)

'Nineteen long winters when God and his Angels slept.'

As daughter of Henry I, Matilda was the legitimate heir to the throne, but had spent most of her life abroad, and the Barons did not relish being ruled by a woman. Matilda's cousin, Stephen, grandson of William the Conqueror, reached England and had himself crowned before Matilda had even left Normandy.

1135 ~ Flying buttresses appear in France

1139–53 ~ Matilda's invasion of England leads to civil war: the Anarchy

1140 ~ Arabic numerals adopted in the West

1141 ~ The Battle of Lincoln, Stephen seized and imprisoned at Bristol

1141 ~ Stephen released in exchange for Matilda's captured half-brother

1142 ~ Stephen lays siege to Oxford Castle, but Matilda escapes

1142–8 ~ Stephen regains power

1147 ~ The Second Crusade

THE HOUSE OF PLANTAGENET
THE REIGN OF HENRY II
(1154–89)

Son of Matilda and Geoffrey of Anjou, and grandson of Henry I, Henry enjoyed vast continental estates, inheriting Anjou, Maine, Normandy and Touraine from his family, while also gaining Aquitaine, Gascony, Poitou and Brittany through dynastic marriage. After his succession to the English throne, Henry ruled an empire in Britain and south-west France greater than any English king before him, owning lands that would preoccupy his successors for generations. Henry's personal badge, a sprig of broom in his helmet, in French *plante à genêt*, gave rise to the dynastic name Plantagenet. During his reign, trial by jury became more commonplace.

12th Century

Coloured statue of Henry II in St Wilfred's Minster, Ripon, wearing a sprig of broom in his crown.

1154 ~ Work starts on York Minster

Nineteen great cathedrals were eventually built, containing holy relics or the remains of saints. These massive works of art also housed the Bishop's throne and were magnificent statements of churchly power and relative human frailty.

1167 ~ Oxford University founded
1169–70 ~ Richard de Clare, Strongbow, begins the conquest of Ireland

1155 ~ Frederick of Barbarossa proclaimed Holy Roman Emperor
1155 ~ Pope Adrian IV (Nicholas Breakspear, the only English Pope) grants Ireland to Henry II of England

1163 ~ Work starts on the Cathedral of Notre-Dame, Paris

Britain

12th Century

1170 ~ Thomas Beckett, the Archbishop of Canterbury, murdered

A friend of the king, Beckett was a royal appointment who nevertheless took the side of the church at the expense of the crown:

'Will no one rid me of this turbulent Priest!'
King Henry II

A wall painting in Bramley Church, Hants, showing Henry II's four knights hacking Beckett to death.

1174 ~ Work starts on Wells Cathedral

1174 ~ The Leaning Tower of Pisa completed

1187 ~ Saladin, the Sultan of Egypt, takes Jerusalem

THE REIGN OF RICHARD I, THE LION HEART (1189–99)

1190–4 ~ The Lion Heart on crusade

1193 ~ Richard imprisoned in Austria

1190 ~ The Teutonic Knights established in Acre, Palestine

1190 ~ The Third Crusade, fails to recapture Jerusalem

1192 ~ Yoromito Minamoto proclaimed Shogun of Japan

Opposite: Richard the Lionheart embarks on the Third Crusade. He fought his way to within twelve miles of Jerusalem, but never took it.

1194 TO 1208

12th ~13th Century

Stained glass depiction of Charlemagne leaving for Spain in Chartres Cathedral.

1194 ~ The king ransomed for 150,000 gold marks, the equivalent of two years' taxes, impoverishing many – those unable to pay the taxes fled beyond the law – giving rise to the legend of Robin Hood

1194 ~ Chartres Cathedral begun

'The Devil is out. Look to yourself.'
THE KING OF FRANCE TO JOHN, ON LEARNING OF KING RICHARD'S RELEASE

1195–99 ~ Richard at war in France

THE REIGN OF JOHN, LACKLAND, SOFTSWORD (1199–1216)

1200 ~ The sheep population, 'half the wealth of England', reaches six million

1202–04 ~ John loses Normandy and Anjou in wars with Philip II of France

1208–14 ~ The Pope imposes an interdict on England, forbidding the ministration of the Sacraments

1200 ~ The University of Paris founded
1201 ~ The Fourth Crusade

1204 ~ Constantinople sacked by the Crusaders
1208–14 ~ The Albigensian Crusade

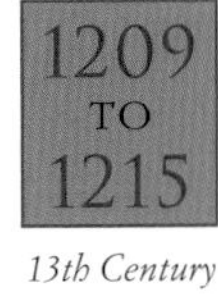

13th Century

1209 ~ Cambridge University founded

1209 ~ The Pope excommunicates King John

1210 ~ China invaded by the Mongol Genghis Khan

1210 ~ The Franciscans founded by St Francis of Assisi

1212 ~ The Children's Crusade

St Francis with Pope Honorius III. He was canonized two years after his death in 1226.

1214 ~ The Battle of Bouvines, John loses his empire in France

Having lost much of his land to Philip II of France, King John took an army over the Channel in an attempt to reclaim his losses. Instead he lost what remained, adding to the Barons' discontent.

1215 ~ Civil war

1215 ~ The Barons force King John to accept the Magna Carta:

1215 ~ St Dominic founds the Dominicans

'To no man will we sell, or deny, or delay right or justice.'
THE MAGNA CARTA, CLAUSE 40

THE REIGN OF HENRY III
(1216–72)

1220 ~ Work starts on Salisbury Cathedral

1221–4 ~ Dominicans and Franciscans arrive in England

1240 ~ The death of Llewellyn I ap Gruffydd of Wales

1240 ~ The King's Great Council becomes known as Parliament

1249 ~ University College, the first Oxford college, founded

1258 ~ The Provisions of Oxford forced on the king, he agrees to summon a Parliament of the Church, Nobles and Commoners

1264 ~ Henry renounces the Provisions, provoking the Barons' War, led by his brother-in-law Simon de Montfort, self-styled 'Steward of England', who captures Henry at the Battle of Lewes

1265 ~ The Battle of Evesham. Henry's son, Edward, defeats and kills de Montfort:

1222 ~ The University of Padua founded

1224 ~ Genghis Khan leads his Mongols into Europe

1232 ~ The first military use of rockets in China

1234 ~ The Chin dynasty brought down by the Mongols

1248 ~ Seville captured from the Moors by Ferdinand of Castile

1250–1570 ~ The Marmelukes rule Egypt

1260 ~ Kubla Khan becomes Emperor of Mongolia

1267 ~ Thomas Aquinas's *Summa Theologica*

'God have mercy on our souls for our bodies are theirs.'

Simon de Montfort

BRITAIN | ABROAD

1267 ~ Roger Bacon's *Opus Maius*, a treatise on the sciences

1271 ~ Venetian explorer Marco Polo leaves for China

13th Century

THE REIGN OF EDWARD I, LONGSHANKS, HAMMER OF THE SCOTS (1272–1307)

c. **1277** ~ The Cross of St George established as the national flag

1281 ~ Peterhouse, the first Cambridge college, founded
1281 ~ The death of Llewellyn II ap Gruffydd of Wales

From the departure of the Romans in 409 to the arrival of the Normans in 1066, Wales had been a patchwork of tribal kingdoms. Over the next 200 years the Normans gradually took control of the South until Edward decided to absorb Wales into his kingdom.

1282–3 ~ Edward conquers Wales and embarks on castle building including Caernarvon and Harlech
1284 ~ The Statute of Wales, brings Wales under English control

St George in golden armour with a red cross on his shield. He was a Roman officer martyred during the Diocletion persecution near Lydda.

1288 TO 1306

13th ~ 14th Century

1290 ~ The Expulsion of the Jews from England

1295 ~ Edward's Model Parliament includes the Church, Nobles and Commoners; representatives from the Cities and Boroughs
1296 ~ Edward invades Scotland and takes the Stone of Destiny from Scone to Westminster

The rival kingdoms of Scotland were never properly occupied by the Romans. They were finally united under Kenneth MacAlpin in 844. His descendants ruled until the heir to the throne, Margaret, died on her journey from Norway in 1290. When 13 rivals claimed the throne, Edward of England, whose son had been betrothed to Margaret, mediated. He chose John Balliol, but when he couldn't control him, Edward took matters into his own hands.

1297 ~ The Battle of Stirling Bridge, the Scots led by William Wallace defeat the English
1298 ~ The Battle of Falkirk, Edward defeats Wallace

c. **1300** ~ The longbow invented
1300 ~ The sheep population reaches 18 million (three sheep to every human)
1301 ~ Having promised the Welsh a 'prince who spoke no English', King Edward invests his heir as Prince of Wales, a babe in arms, as yet unable to speak at all
1306 ~ Robert the Bruce crowned King of Scotland

1288–1919 ~ The Ottomans assume power in Turkey

Robert the Bruce at Bannockburn. His body is buried at Dumfernline. His heart was to be buried in Jerusalem, but got no further than Melrose.

c. **1300** ~ Gunpowder reaches the West

Britain	Abroad
1306 ~ The Rebellion of Robert the Bruce:	**1306** ~ The Expulsion of the Jews from France

'If at first you don't succeed,
try, try again.'

14th Century

THE REIGN OF EDWARD II,
Edward of Caernarvon
(1307–27)

1307 ~ Dante's *The Divine Comedy*

1309 ~ Pope Clement V leaves Rome to rule from Avignon

1311 ~ Edward antagonizes the Barons by his favouritism towards Piers Gaveston, whom the Barons force into exile

1312 ~ Gaveston executed on his return to England

1314 ~ The Battle of Bannockburn, the Scots defeat the English

1320 ~ The Declaration of Arbroath made by the Scots:

'It is in truth not for glory nor riches nor honours that we are fighting but for freedom – for that alone which no honest man gives up but with life itself.'

1321–2 ~ Civil War, led by the king's cousin, Thomas, Earl of Lancaster

1322 ~ The Battle of Boroughbridge, Edward subdues the rebels and kills Lancaster

1325 ~ The Aztecs settle in the Valley of Mexico, founding the city of Tenochtitlán

1326–7 ~ Edward's estranged French wife, Isabella, and her exiled lover, Roger Mortimer, Earl of March, invade England from France and murder the king

1330 TO 1346

14th Century

THE REIGN OF EDWARD III, 'King of the Sea' (1327–77)

'The affairs that concern the King and the estate of his realm shall be directed by the common counsel of his realm and in no other wise.'

Proclamation issued by Edward after the arrest of Mortimer

Edward III inherited an unstable throne, his father having provoked the Barons through his favouritism and incompetence, his mother having deposed her own husband. After his death, the Queen Mother and her lover, Mortimer, controlled the King, Edward III, until he came of age in 1330.

1330 ~ Isabella imprisoned; Mortimer arrested and executed

1334 ~ Work starts on Giotto's Tower, the campanile or bell tower of Florence Cathedral

1337 ~ Edward claims the throne of France

1337 ~ Edward invades France. The start of the Hundred Years War:

'The King appoynted his souldiers to wear white coats or jackets with a red crosse before and behind over their armoure, that it was not onely a comely but a stately sight to behold the English Battles, like a rising sunne, to glitter farre off in the pure hew; when the souldiers of other nations in their baser weedes could not be discerned.'

1340 ~ The Battle of Sluys, the English defeat the French at sea

1346 ~ The Battle of Crécy, victory over the French:

'Let the boy win his spurs.'

Edward of his son, the Black Prince, during the battle

14th Century

1346 ~ The Battle of Neville's Cross, victory over the Scots

1347 ~ Calais falls to the English

1348–9 ~ The Black Death kills one third of the population (over 2 million) in two years

1350 ~ *Sir Gawain and the Green Knight*

The Green Knight picks up his own severed head after Sir Gawain has lopped it off.

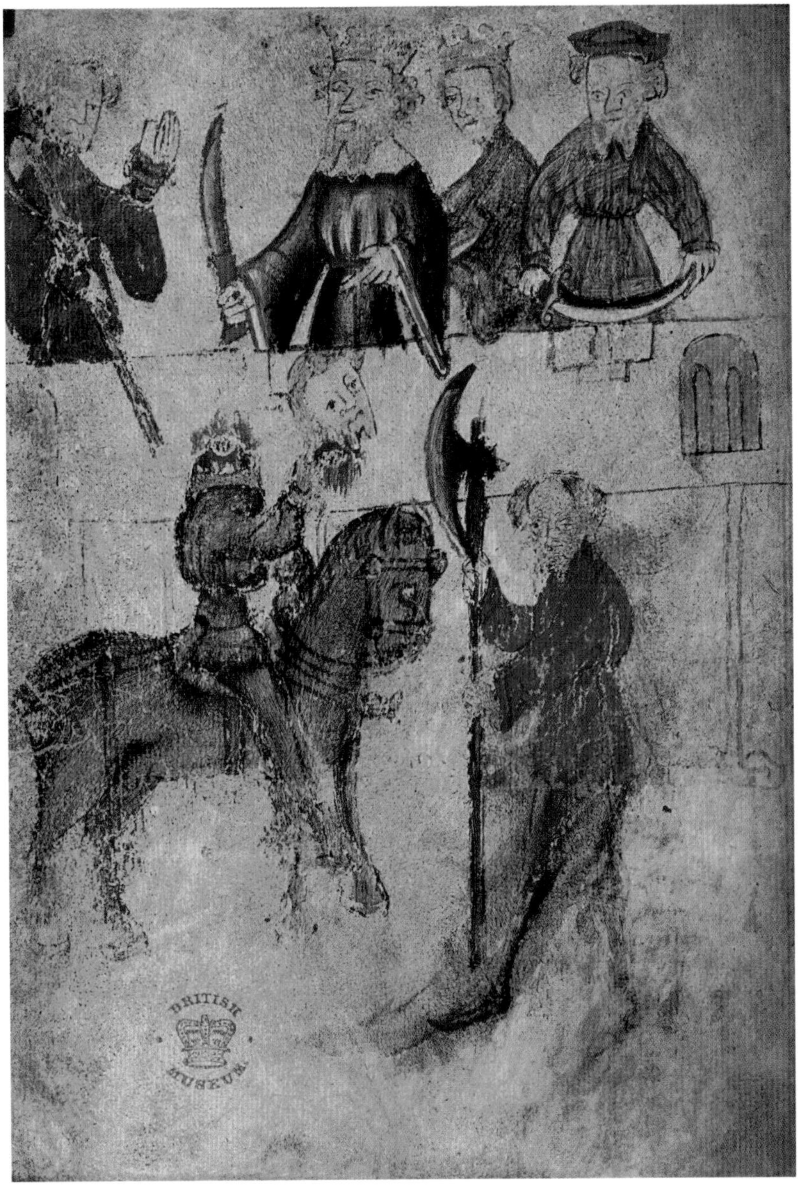

Opposite: Edward III with The Earl of Flanders. His tact and gift for diplomacy allowed him to put internal feuding aside and take on France and Scotland.

1351 TO 1369

14th Century

Britain

1351 ~ The Statute of Labourers outlaws wage rises in response to the labour shortage caused by the Black Death

1356 ~ The Battle of Poitiers, the English capture Jean II of France

1360 ~ The Treaty of Brétigny, Edward renounces his claim to Normandy in exchange for Aquitaine and Calais

1362 ~ Parliament opens in English which also replaces French in the courts

1369 ~ France retakes Aquitaine, renewing hostilities

Abroad

1356 ~ The Ottoman Turks attack Europe

1366 ~ Petrarch writes 365 love sonnets (one a day) to Laura

Francesco Petrarca, or Petrarch, whose writing was influenced by Dante and whose interest in Ancient Greek and Roman authors helped revive interest in the classics.

1368–1644 ~ The Ming Dynasty, China

14th Century

1370 ~ The Black Prince, 'the Comfort of England', sacks Limoges

1376 ~ The Good Parliament elects a 'Speaker' for the first time and urges the king to:

'Live off his own.'

1376 ~ The death of the Black Prince:

'Such as thou art, so once was I.
As I am now, so thou wilt be.'
Inscription on the
Black Prince's tomb

Edward, Prince of Wales, the 'Black Prince', who was 'styled black by terror of his arms'.

The Reign of Richard II, Richard of Bordeaux (1377–99)

1377 ~ John Wyclif, 'the Morning Star of the Reformation', preaches against the Pope, monks and friars, attracting followers to the Lollard movement

1380 ~ John Wyclif translates the Bible

1381 ~ The Poll Tax, levied on everyone over 14

1377 ~ Pope Gregory XI returns to Rome

1378–1415 ~ The Great Papal Schism, rival Popes at Avignon and Rome

14th Century

1381 ~ The Peasants' Revolt

'When Adam delved and Eve span who then was the gentleman?'
JOHN BALL

'You shall have no other Captain but I.'
THE YOUNG KING RICHARD FEARLESSLY RIDING INTO THE MOB OF HOSTILE 'PEASANTS' AFTER THEIR LEADER, WAT TYLER, HAD BEEN CUT DOWN BY THE KING'S MEN

1382 ~ Winchester College founded by William of Wykeham, Bishop of Winchester

1387 ~ Chaucer's *The Canterbury Tales*:

1385 ~ The Visconti family assume power in Milan

'When April with his showers sweet
The drought of March hath pierced to the root
And bathed every vein in such liquor
Of which virtue engendered is the flower.'

This 14th-century edition of Boccaccio became the basis of Chaucer's 'The Knight's Tale'.

1393 ~ The Ottoman Turks take Bulgaria

1395 ~ The Mongol Golden Horde vanquished by Tamberlane

1396 ~ The Peace of Paris, England retains only Calais and part of Gascony

1397–8 ~ Richard kills or banishes leading nobles who try to curb his powers

1399 ~ One of the exiled nobles, Henry of Bolingbroke, John of Gaunt's son, invades England in Richard's absence, reclaims his Lancastrian estates, and usurps the throne, forcing Richard to abdicate. Richard dies in prison

THE HOUSE OF LANCASTER
THE REIGN OF HENRY IV,
Henry of Bolingbroke
(1399–1413)

1400–5 ~ The Rebellion of Owain Glyndwr, self-styled Prince of Wales

c. **1400** ~ The Renaissance begins in Italy

Although of royal descent, Henry IV had seized power by force, casting doubts on his right to the throne. The most potent challenge arose in the North, from the Percys of Northumberland, led by the Earl and his son Henry 'Hotspur'. In Wales, Owen Glendower exploited the uncertainties to win support from Northumberland and the French.

1403 ~ Defeat and death of Hotspur at Shrewsbury

1405 ~ Richard Scrope's rebellion quashed

1405–33 ~ Chinese fleets reach Africa, the Persian Gulf and south-east Asia

1408 ~ Donatello's *David*

15th Century

THE REIGN OF HENRY V, HENRY OF MONMOUTH (1413–22)

1415 ~ The Battle of Agincourt, victory over the French:

'Cry "God for Harry! England and St George!"'

1417–19 ~ Henry reconquers Normandy, reaching Paris in 1419

A contemporary map of Africa.

1420 ~ The Treaty of Troyes recognizes King Henry as heir to the throne of France. He marries Catherine of Valois, daughter of the French King Charles VI

1421–2 ~ Henry returns to France, where he puts down opposition, but dies of dysentery at Vincennes

1420 ~ The Portuguese, under Prince Henry the Navigator, start exploring West Africa

THE REIGN OF HENRY VI (1422–61)

1422 ~ The infant Henry succeeds to the English and French thrones

1423 ~ The death of Dick Whittington, four times Lord Mayor of London

1423–4 ~ English victories at the Battles of Cravant and Verneuil

1428 ~ The English besiege Orléans

Joan of Arc leads the French into battle. Regarded by the French as a saint, the English condemned her as a witch.

1429 ~ Joan of Arc relieves Orléans

1431 ~ Joan of Arc burnt at the stake

1430s ~ Flemish artist van Eyck refines the art of painting in oil

1434 ~ The Medici family assume power in Florence

1436 ~ The French recapture Paris from the English

15th Century

Britain

1440 ~ Eton College founded

1444 ~ The Treaty of Tours, a five-year truce

1450 ~ Normany lost to the French
1450 ~ John Cade's Rebellion

Abroad

1438 ~ The Inca Empire stretches from Ecuador to Chile

A French map of Constantinople in 1420.

Britain

1453 ~ Gascony falls to the French, ending the Hundred Years War. England retains only Calais

1453–4 ~ After Henry suffers a spate of insanity, Richard Duke of York acts as Protector, causing unrest between the rival royal houses of Lancaster and York

1454–5 ~ Rivalry intensifies between the two factions, symbolized by the heraldic white rose of York and red rose of Lancaster

Abroad

1453 ~ The Ottoman Turks take Constantinople

1454 ~ Gutenberg uses moveable type

1455 ~ The Battle of St Albans, the Wars of the Roses between the Yorkists and Lancastrians begin

1455 ~ The Lancastrian leader, Edmund Beaufort, Duke of Somerset, falls on the field of St Albans

1460 ~ Henry is seized by the Yorkists, and forced to acknowledge Richard of York as his heir

1460 ~ York falls at Wakefield

1461 ~ The Lancastrians recapture Henry, but the Yorkists depose him again at the Battle of Towton, led by York's son, Edward, who is crowned Edward IV, forcing Henry, his wife and son to flee to Scotland

1458 ~ The Aztec Empire stretches from Mexico to Guatemala

Henry VI presents a sword to The Earl of Shrewsbury. In his 19-year reign he would need all the war-like friends he could find.

Britain | Abroad

15th Century

THE HOUSE OF YORK
THE REIGN OF EDWARD IV
(1461–83)

1465 ~ Henry captured by the Yorkists

1469 ~ Sir Thomas Malory's *Le Morte d'Arthur*:

1469 ~ Spain united by the marriage of Ferdinand of Aragon and Isabella of Castile

'Whoso pulleth out this sword of this stone and anvil is rightwise King born of all England.'

1470 ~ Warwick the Kingmaker, Earl of Warwick, deposes Edward, who flees to Burgundy

1471 ~ Henry briefly restored to the throne by Warwick

Queen Guinevere from the Aubrey Beardsley edition of Le Morte D' Arthur.

1471 ~ Edward IV returns, killing Warwick at Barnet, and defeating Queen Margaret at Tewkesbury and killing her son
1471 ~ Henry VI murdered in the Tower of London
1474 ~ William Caxton produces the first printed book in English

1479 ~ The Spanish Inquisition established

THE REIGN OF EDWARD V
ONE OF THE MURDERED 'PRINCES IN THE TOWER'
(1483)

1483 ~ On the death of Edward IV, his two young sons, Edward V and Richard of York, are put in the Tower for 'safe keeping' by their uncle Richard, Duke of Gloucester. The 'Princes in the Tower' were never seen again

THE REIGN OF RICHARD III
CROUCHBACK
(1483–5)

1483 ~ Richard puts down a revolt led by Henry Stafford, Duke of Buckingham
1484 ~ The king's only son and heir dies, weakening his dynastic position
1485 ~ The Battle of Bosworth, Henry Tudor, the Lancastrian rival to the throne, returns from exile to challenge Richard who dies on the field of battle

Richard III. His hump may have had more to do with propaganda than reality.

1486 TO 1508

15th ~ 16th Century

THE HOUSE OF TUDOR
THE REIGN OF HENRY VII
(1485–1509)

1486 ~ By marrying Elizabeth of York, Henry unites the Houses of Lancaster and York, so ending the Wars of the Roses

Opposite: The flood from the Sistine Chapel.

1487 ~ The Rebellion of Lambert Simnel, claiming to be the Earl of Warwick, put down at the Battle of Stoke. Simnel, a baker's son, is given a job in the Royal Kitchens

1487 ~ Portuguese explorer Bartholomew Diaz rounds the Cape of Good Hope

1491 ~ The Rebellion of Perkin Warbeck, claiming to be one of the missing Princes in the Tower

1492 ~ Christopher Columbus reaches the West Indies

1493 ~ The Pope divides the New World between Spain and Portugal

1497 ~ Leonardo da Vinci's *The Last Supper*

1498 ~ Vasco da Gama reaches Calicut, India

Christopher Columbus confronts the Carib Indians in the West Indies.

1499 ~ John Cabot reaches Newfoundland

1503 ~ Leonardo's *Mona Lisa*

1508 ~ Michelangelo starts work on the ceiling of the Sistine Chapel, Rome

THE REIGN OF HENRY VIII
(1509–47)

Despite his early defence of the Pope and attacks on Protestantism, Henry VIII eventually broke with Rome when his first wife failed to produce a male heir and the Pope refused to grant him a divorce.

The wife he divorced, Catherine of Aragon, produced one daughter, Mary Tudor, later known as 'Bloody Mary'. Henry's second wife, Anne Boleyn, whom he executed, had one daughter, the future Elizabeth I. Henry's third wife, Jane Seymour, died after giving birth to his only legitimate son, the future Edward VI. The King's marriage to his fourth wife, Anne of Cleves, was dissolved. Catherine Howard, Henry's fifth wife, was executed. The King's final and sixth wife, Catherine Parr, survived him.

1513 ~ War with France and Scotland

1513 ~ The Battle of Flodden, the English defeat the Scots

1516 ~ Sir Thomas More's *Utopia*

1509 ~ Erasmus writes *In Praise of Folly*

1516 ~ Macchiavelli's *The Prince*

1517 ~ Martin Luther nails his 95 Theses to the Church door in Wittenburg, Germany

1518 ~ Titian, 'the father of modern painting', completes *The Assumption of the Virgin*

1519 ~ Hernando Cortés leads his Spaniards into Mexico

Martin Luther gave up all hope of reforming the Catholic church in 1530 and set up a separate Protestant Church.

16th Century

Britain

1520 ~ Henry meets King Francis I of France at the Field of the Cloth of Gold

1521 ~ Henry given the title *Fidei Defensor* (Defender of the Faith) by the Pope

1526 ~ William Tyndale's English translation of the New Testament:

Abroad

1520–1 Portuguese explorer Magellan circumnavigates the globe

1521 ~ The fall of the city of Tenochtitlán in Mexico to the Spaniards, the end of the Aztec Empire

1521 ~ The Reformation begins with the Diet of Worms

1526 ~ Babur, Prince of Fergana, founds the Mughal Empire in India

'If God spare my life, ere many years I will cause a boy that driveth the plough shall know more of the scriptures than though doest.'

King Henry VIII – The frontispiece from the Bible said to have been designed by Hans Holbein

16th Century

Britain

1527 ~ Henry decides to divorce his first wife, Catherine of Aragon

1529 ~ The Fall of Cardinal Wolsey:

Abroad

1527 ~ The sack of Rome by Holy Roman Emperor Charles V

1529 ~ The Ottoman Turks attack Vienna

'Had I but served God as diligently as I have served the King, he would not have given me over in my grey hairs.'

Britain

1533 ~ Henry marries Anne Boleyn

1534 ~ The Act of Supremacy, abolishes the Pope's authority in England

1535 ~ The first English translation of The Bible completed by Miles Coverdale

Abroad

1533 ~ The Inca Empire brought down by Spanish conquistadore Francisco Pizzaro

1534 ~ The Jesuits, the Society of Jesus, founded by the Spanish saint, Ignatius of Loyola

1535 ~ French explorer Jacques Cartier reaches the St Lawrence River in North America

1535 ~ Sir Thomas More and Bishop John Fisher executed:

'I pray you, master Lieutenant, see me safe up, and my coming down let me shift for myself.'
THOMAS MORE AT HIS EXECUTION

1536 ~ Anne Boleyn executed
1536–9 ~ With the Dissolution of the Monasteries, shrines and relics are destroyed, and monasteries repressed, closed, plundered and sold off to swell the king's coffers

1536 ~ The Pilgrimage of Grace, an armed uprising in opposition to Henry's changes to the church and monastic closure, savagely repressed
1536 ~ Wales incorporated into political union with England

Opposite: At one time the most powerful man in England, Cardinal Wolsey's failure to engineer the King's divorce proved his downfall.

1538 ~ Hans Holbein's *Anne of Cleves*
1538 ~ Every Parish ordered to buy a copy of the English Great Bible

1540 ~ The execution of Thomas Cromwell
1541 ~ John Knox leads the Calvinist Reformation in Scotland

Sir Thomas More with his chain of office on his knees.

1539 ~ The death of Guru Nanak, founder of Sikhism

16th Century

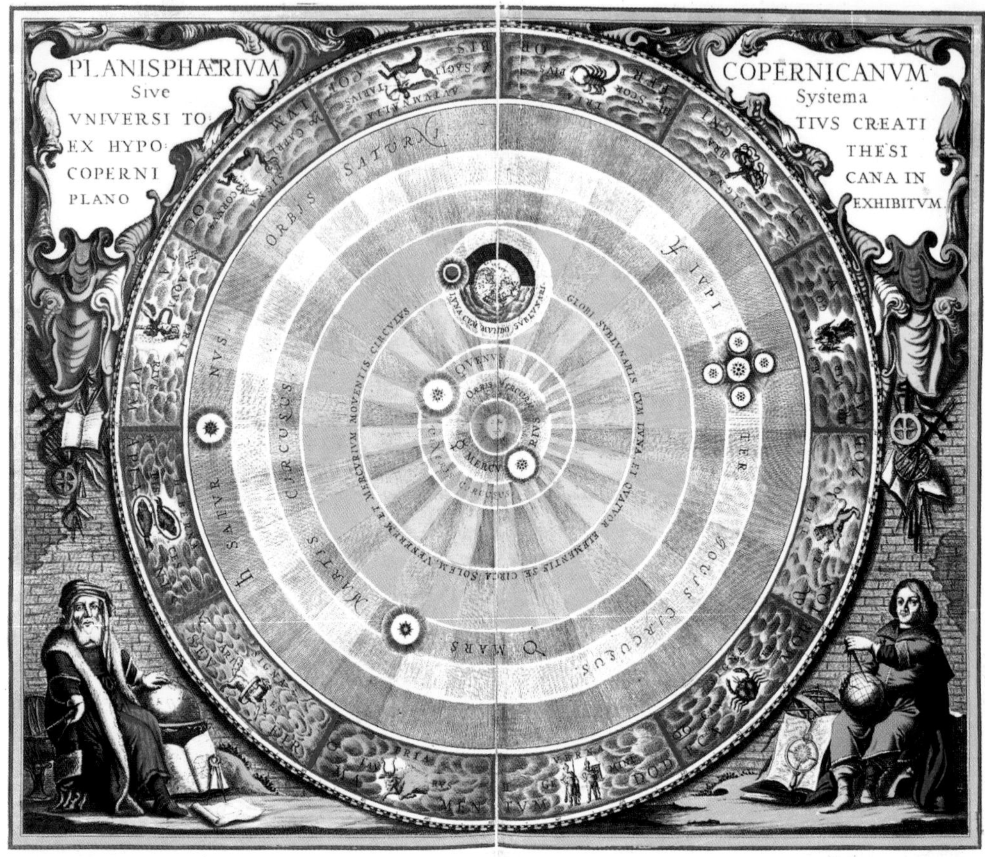

The Universe according to Copernicus.

1542 ~ The Battle of Solway Moss, the English defeat the Scots

1543 ~ Polish astronomer, Copernicus, argues that the Earth orbits the Sun in *De revolutionibus*

THE REIGN OF EDWARD VI
(1547–53)

Though Henry VIII had broken with Rome, he remained wary of Protestantism. Henry's son, Edward VI, had no such doubts and was fully committed to a Protestant kingdom.

1547–9 ~ Somerset's Protectorate, King Edward guided by his uncle, Edward Seymour, Duke of Somerset

1547 ~ Ivan the Terrible of Russia adopts the title Tsar

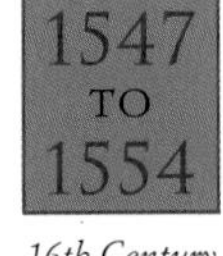

1547–9 ~ Robert Ket's rebellion in Norfolk put down by John Dudley, Earl of Warwick:

'He hath conceived a wonderful hate against all gentlemen.'

1549–53 ~ Somerset replaced by John Dudley, Earl of Warwick, later Duke of Northumberland

1549 ~ The first Book of Common Prayer:

'It is a thing plainly repugnant to the word of God, and the custom of the Primitive Church, to have publick prayer in the church, or to minister the sacraments, in a tongue not understanded of the people.'

The 24th Article of Religion

1550–1650 ~ The Counter Reformation stimulates reform within the Roman Church

1550s ~ French Protestant John Calvin establishes the Reformed Church in Geneva

THE REIGN OF LADY JANE GREY (1553)

When it was clear Edward VI's illness would lead to his death, he nominated a fellow Protestant, Lady Jane Grey, as his heir. But the English people regarded Henry VIII's eldest daughter, Mary Tudor, as the rightful Queen, and rallied to her standard. Lady Jane Grey ruled for just nine days in July.

THE REIGN OF MARY I, BLOODY MARY (1553–8)

Mary Tudor was daughter to Henry VIII and Catherine of Aragon and a devout Catholic. Her brutal attempt to return England to the Catholic fold alienated her subjects and earned her the title 'Bloody Mary'.

1554 ~ The execution of Lady Jane Grey

1554 ~ Mary marries Philip of Spain, the heir to the Spanish throne

16th Century

1554 ~ Sir Thomas Wyatt's rebellion in protest at the Queen's Spanish marriage

1554–6 ~ England reunited with Rome

A stained glass window in St Mary's Church, Bury St Edmunds, in memory of Queen Mary I and given by Queen Victoria.

1555 ~ Protestant Bishops Hugh Latimer and Nicholas Ridley burnt at the stake:

'Be of good comfort, Master Ridley, and play the man. We shall this day light such a candle by God's Grace in England, as I trust shall never be put out.'

HUGH LATIMER

1556 ~ Philip becomes King of Spain
1556 ~ Protestant Archbishop Thomas Cranmer burnt at the stake

1558 ~ The loss of Calais, the last remnant of a once proud empire in France:

1556–1605 ~ Akbar the Great rules India

'When I am dead and opened you shall find "Calais" lying in my heart.'

QUEEN MARY

THE REIGN OF ELIZABETH I, THE VIRGIN QUEEN (1558–1603)

'This is the Lord's doing and it is marvellous in our eyes.'
PSALM 118, QUOTED BY QUEEN ELIZABETH ON LEARNING OF HER ACCESSION

After the agony of Bloody Mary's reign, Elizabeth refrained from persecuting Catholics but embraced Protestantism as a patriotic necessity.

1560s ~ Flemish weavers settle in the south east
1562 ~ The Church of England's Thirty-Nine Articles of Religion:

'There is but one living and true God, everlasting, without body, parts, or passions; of infinite power, wisdom, and goodness; the Maker and Preserver of all things both visible and invisible. And in unity of the Godhead there be three persons, of one substance, power and eternity; the Father, the Son, and The Holy Ghost.'
THE FIRST ARTICLE OF RELIGION

1563 ~ John Foxe's *Book of Martyrs*
1565 ~ Sir Walter Raleigh brings tobacco and potatoes from the New World

1566 ~ Protestant Holland rebels against rule by Catholic Spain

Sir Walter Raleigh, explorer, courtier and poet, and a favourite of Elizabeth I. He had no such appeal to the passionate anti-smoker, King James.

BRITAIN | ABROAD

16th Century

1568 ~ Mary Queen of Scots flees to England

1570 ~ Elizabeth excommunicated by the Pope:

'I would not open windows into men's souls.'

1570 ~ Palladio's *The Four Books of Architecture*

1570 ~ Leonard Digges invents the theodolite

1571 ~ The Battle of Lepanto ends the Turkish threat to Europe from the sea

1572 ~ The St Bartholomew's Day Massacre of French Huguenots (Protestants) in Paris

1574–1604 ~ The Sikhs build the Golden Temple at Amritsar, India

1577–80 ~ Sir Francis Drake's first voyage round the world:

'There must be a beginning of any great matter, but the continuing unto the end until it be thoroughly finished yields the true glory.'

1584 ~ English settlers planted in Ulster

1587 ~ Mary Stuart, Queen of Scots, executed

Queen Elizabeth holds the Royal Orb and Sceptre and wears one of her famous jewel-encrusted dresses. On her death she had over 300 of them.

Britain | Abroad

16th Century

1587 ~ Drake's raid on Cadiz, home port of the Spanish navy:

'I have singed the King of Spain's beard.'

1588 ~ The defeat of the Spanish Armada:

Sir Francis Drake captures Valdez's great galleon.

'There is plenty of time to win this game and thrash the Spaniards too.'

Drake's response during a game of bowls to the sighting of the Armada

'I know I have the body of a weak and feeble woman, but I have the heart and stomach of a King, and a King of England too!'

Queen Elizabeth to her troops at Tilbury

1590 ~ Edmund Spencer's *Faerie Queene*; Christopher Marlowe's *Tamburlaine the Great*

MR. WILLIAM
SHAKESPEARES
COMEDIES,
HISTORIES, &
TRAGEDIES.

Publiſhed according to the True Originall Copies.

LONDON
Printed by Iſaac Iaggard, and Ed. Blount. 1623.

Britain | Abroad

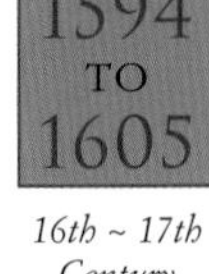
16th ~ 17th Century

1594 ~ William Shakespeare's *Romeo and Juliet*

1598 ~ Shakespeare's *Henry V*

1598 ~ The Edict of Nantes grants tolerance to French Protestants

1600 ~ The East India Company founded

1601 ~ The Earl of Essex's rebellion

1601 ~ The Golden Speech:

'Though God hath raised me high, yet this I count the glory of my crown: that I have reigned with your loves.'

Queen Elizabeth's Golden Speech

1601 ~ Shakespeare's *Hamlet*

1603 ~ The death of Queen Elizabeth:

'All my possessions for a moment of time.'

Her last words

THE HOUSE OF STUART
THE REIGN OF JAMES I (VI OF SCOTLAND), THE 'WISEST FOOL IN CHRISTENDOM' (1603–25)

Son of Mary Queen of Scots, James had been King of Scotland since 1567.

'The state of Monarchy is the supremest thing upon earth...even by God himself they (Kings) are called Gods.'

King James

1605 ~ The Gunpowder Plot:

'A desperate disease requires a dangerous remedy.'

Guy Fawkes

1605 ~ Miguel de Cervantes's *Don Quixote*

Opposite: A portrait of William Shakespeare who was born and died on St George's Day, and who added at least 7,000 words and phrases to the English language.

BRITAIN ~ ABROAD

17th Century

1606 ~ The Union Flag adopted as the national flag

1606 ~ The Italians discover the secret of Chocolate, breaking the Spanish monopoly

UNION FLAG

The Union Flag before the incorporation of St Patrick's Flag in 1801.

1607 ~ Jamestown founded in America, by the Virginia Company

1607–9 ~ Rebellion in Ireland over settlement by Protestants

1608 ~ The first East India Company ships reach Surat, India

1609 ~ Galileo perfects his telescope

1611 ~ The Authorised or King James version of the Bible:

'In the beginning God created the Heaven and the Earth.'

1616 ~ The death of Shakespeare

1618 ~ Sir Walter Raleigh executed:

'Tis a sharp remedy but a sure one for all ills.'

SIR WALTER RALEIGH ON TRYING THE EDGE OF THE AXE

1618 ~ The Thirty Years War begins with the Defenestration of Prague

1619 ~ African slaves arrive in Virginia

1620 ~ The Pilgrim Fathers depart for New England

1621 ~ 'The Corante', the first English newspaper, published

The Pilgrim Fathers sailed from Plymouth in the 180-ton Mayflower *on the 6 September 1620 and reached Cape Cod on 11 November.*

1624 ~ Frans Hals's *The Laughing Cavalier*

THE REIGN OF CHARLES I (1625–49)

1624–30 ~ England at war with Spain

1626–9 ~ England at war with France

1626 ~ New Amsterdam (later New York) established by the Dutch

1628 ~ William Harvey explains the circulation of blood

1628 ~ The Petition of Right forced on Charles, specifying the monarch's duties towards his subjects and Parliament's right to discuss such issues in the future

1628 ~ The Huguenots, besieged at La Rochelle, surrender to Cardinal Richelieu

1629 ~ Parliament dissolved by the King

1632 ~ Anthony Van Dyck becomes royal Painter-in-Ordinary

1632–53 ~ Shah Jahan builds the Taj Mahal

1633 ~ Galileo persuaded by the Inquisition to recant his belief in the earth circling the sun

17th Century

Britain	Abroad
1635 ~ Peter Paul Rubens completes the ceiling of the Banqueting House in Whitehall Palace	**1635** ~ The Académie Française founded in Paris
	1636 ~ Harvard University founded in Boston
	1637 ~ The Tulip Crash in Holland
1638 ~ The Scots revolt over Bishop Laud's attempt to impose the Anglican Prayer Book on the Kirk	
1640 ~ The Short Parliament	
1640–60 ~ The Long Parliament	
1641 ~ The Grand Remonstrance, Parliament rebukes the King and demands to take over government	
1642 ~ Attempted arrest of the Five Members of Parliament:	**1642** ~ Tasmania discovered by Dutchman Abel Tasman

'I have neither eyes to see nor tongue to speak in this place but as the House is pleased to direct me.'

Speaker Lenthall's response to Charles's demand for the five MPs

'I see the birds have flown.'

Charles I on finding the five MPs gone

Britain	Abroad
1642 ~ Outbreak of the Civil War, King Charles and his Royalists fight the Parliamentarians over the respective powers of the King and Parliament	**1642** ~ Montreal founded by the French in Canada
	1642 ~ Rembrandt's *The Night Watch*
1642 ~ The Battle of Edgehill, the Royalist Cavaliers defeat the Parliamentarians:	

'Your King is your Cause, your Quarrel and your Captain.'

King Charles

'O Lord thou knowest how busy I must be this day. If I forget thee, do not forget me.'

SIR JACOB ASTLEY'S PRAYER ON THE MORNING OF BATTLE

1643 ~ Thomas Browne's *Religio Medici* (Religion of the Physician)

1644 ~ The Battle of Marston Moor The Parliamentary Roundheads defeat the Royalists:

1643 ~ Louis XIV becomes King of France

1644 ~ The Manchus take Peking, establishing the Ch'ing Dynasty

'God made them as stubble to our swords.'

OLIVER CROMWELL

1645 ~ The Battle of Naseby, the New Model Army breaks the Royalist infantry

1647 ~ The Putney Debates:

Oliver Cromwell at Marston Moor. It was not until Naseby that his New Model Army really came into its own.

'The poorest he that is in England hath a life to live as the greatest he.'

COLONEL THOMAS RAINBOROUGH MP

17th Century

1648 ~ George Fox founds the Society of Friends or Quakers:

1648 ~ The Peace of Westphalia ends the Thirty Years War

'All bloody principles and practices, we, as to our own particulars, do utterly deny with all outward wars and strife and fightings with outward weapons, for any end or under any pretence whatsoever. And this is our testament to the whole world.'

BRITAIN | ABROAD

17th Century

1648 ~ The Battle of Preston, Cromwell defeats the Royalists

1649 ~ King Charles executed:

1649 ~ Russian peasants made serfs

'A Subject and A Soveraign are clean different things.'
CHARLES I

'Rebellion to tyrants is obedience to God.'
JUDGE BRADSHAW

'The people, under God, are the source of all just power.'
THE RUMP PARLIAMENT

Opposite: Charles I in the snow. He would request a second shirt at his execution in case the chill should make him shiver and seem afraid.

THE COMMONWEALTH (1649–60)

1649–50 ~ Oliver Cromwell's conquest of Ireland:

'I beseech you, in the bowels of Christ, think it possible you may be mistaken.'
CROMWELL TO THE KIRK OF SCOTLAND, 1650

1650–2 ~ Cromwell's conquest of Scotland

1650s ~ The first Coffee Houses open

Oliver Cromwell carries the Bible on which he tried to base his actions.

1651 TO 1660

17th Century

1651 ~ Thomas Hobbes's *Leviathan or The Matter, Form and Power of a Commonwealth, Ecclesiastical and Civil*:

'The life of man (is) solitary, poore, nasty, brutish and short.'

1651 ~ The Battle of Worcester, Charles II invades England from Scotland, but is defeated by Cromwell and flees to France

1652 ~ Tea arrives in Britain from China

1653 ~ Cromwell proclaimed Lord Protector:

'You have sat too long here for any good you have been doing. Depart, I say, and let us have done with you! In the name of God, go!'
OLIVER CROMWELL TO PARLIAMENT

'Take away that fool's bauble!'
OF THE PARLIAMENTARY MACE

1656 ~ The Jews invited to return

1656 ~ Velazquez paints *Las Meninas*

1658 ~ The death of Oliver Cromwell
On his death, Oliver Cromwell was succeeded by his son Richard, Tumbledown Dick, but it soon became clear he could not control the army. From Holland Charles II offered a free pardon, freedom of religion and pay for the army if allowed to take the throne. General Monck marched his soldiers to London and persuaded Parliament to accept.

1660 ~ The Restoration, the Monarchy restored

THE REIGN OF CHARLES II
(1660–85)

'I am weary of travelling and resolved to go abroad no more.'
Charles II

1660 ~ The Royal Society founded

1662 ~ *The Book of Common Prayer*:

'I pray and beseech you, as many as are here present, to accompany me with a pure heart, and humble voice, unto the throne of the heavenly grace.'

1664–5 ~ The last Great Plague:

'Ring-a-ring-o-roses,
a pocket full of posies,
atishoo, atishoo,
we all fall down.'

'Bring out your dead.'

1664 ~ The Ottoman Turks take Hungary

A plague gravestone of 1666. The Great Fire of London which followed it, is credited with its final disappearance.

1666 ~ The Great Fire of London

1667 ~ A Dutch fleet sails up the River Medway, captures the *Royal Charles*, and sinks three other great ships

17th Century

1667 ~ John Milton's *Paradise Lost*:

> *'Of man's first disobedience, and the fruit*
> *Of that forbidden tree, whose mortal taste*
> *Brought death into the world, and all our woe,*
> *With loss of Eden.'*

1674 ~ England makes peace with the Dutch

1674–1738 ~ The life of 'Turnip' Townshend, champion of four field crop rotation

1677 ~ John Bunyan's *The Pilgrim's Progress*:

> *'As I walked through the wilderness of this world...'*

1674 ~ The Poles elect Jan Sobiewski as King

1677 ~ Racine's *Phèdre*

A scene from The Pilgrim's Progress *in brass at Bunyan Hall in Bedford. Bunyan spent eleven years in prison where he earned a living making tagged laces.*

Charles II returns to England. He said 'The safety, honour and welfare of England do chiefly depend on the navy – and God.'

1679 ~ The Act of Habeas Corpus passed, forcing the State to justify an individual's arrest with the accusation of a recognized criminal offence, and to produce the accused in person before a magistrate within two days

1679 ~ The last dodo killed

Though related to the pigeon, the dodo lost the power of flight, which was not a problem until the Dutch brought predators such as the pig to Mauritius.

1683 ~ Charles survives the Rye House plot
1685 ~ The death of Charles II

1683 ~ The Ottoman Turks lay siege to Vienna
1685 ~ The Revocation of the Edict of Nantes

'Let not poor Nelly starve.'
THE KING'S LAST WORDS, ABOUT HIS MISTRESS NELL GWYN

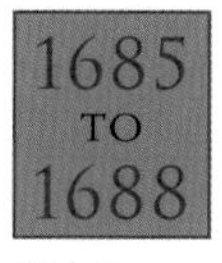

17th Century

THE REIGN OF JAMES II
(1685–8)

1685 ~ The Duke of Monmouth's pitchfork rebellion crushed by royal forces at the Battle of Sedgemoor; Monmouth executed, and the rebels brutally punished at the Bloody Assizes

1687 ~ Isaac Newton's *Principia Mathematica*:

'To every Action there is always opposed an equal Reaction.'

1688 ~ James deposed in the Glorious Revolution

British Protestants were prepared to tolerate a Catholic king, James II, as long as he had no Catholic heirs. James's two eldest daughters, Mary and Anne, were Protestant, but when his new Catholic wife gave birth to a son, British Protestants invited James's daughter Mary and her Protestant husband, Prince William of Orange, to take the throne. When the royal army deserted to William, James II fled to France.

Isaac Newton, who among his other great achievements, also invented the cat flap.

THE REIGN OF WILLIAM AND MARY (1689–1702)

'There is one way never to see your country lost, and that is to die in the last ditch!'
King William

1689 ~ The Bill of Rights

After the vagaries of the Stuart Kings, Parliament was no longer prepared to give the monarch a free hand. William and Mary signed the Bill of Rights which confirmed the right of Parliament to be consulted frequently, and barred Catholics from any official post.

1690 ~ John Locke's *An Essay concerning Human Understanding*:

'No man's knowledge can go beyond his experience.'

1690 ~ The Battle of the Boyne, William defeats James II

1692 ~ Edward Lloyd opens his coffee shop, favoured by insurance brokers
1692 ~ The Massacre of Glencoe, the Campbells slaughter the Macdonalds

1692 ~ Christians granted official tolerance in China

1694 ~ The Bank of England founded

1697–1851 ~ Window Tax levied: two shillings for a house with 6–10 windows, four shillings for 10–20, eight shillings for over 20. Houses with under 6 windows exempt

William III and his wife Mary II, the Protestant daughter of James II.

1698 ~ Thomas Savery patents his mine pump

1698 ~ A list of the prices of Stocks, Shares and Commodities posted at Jonathon's Coffee House in 'Change Alley'

1700–70 ~ 15,000 miles of turnpike roads built, shifting the burden of road maintenance from local parishioners to non-local road users

1700 ~ Scotland bankrupted by the colonization of Darien fiasco, in Panama

1701 ~ The Act of Settlement bars Catholics from the throne, and settles on an appropriate Protestant successor to the crown

1698 ~ Goose-stepping introduced in the Prussian army

18th Century

1701–13 ~ The War of Spanish Succession

When Carlos II of Spain died in 1700, without male heir, Louis XIV of France saw a chance to put his own son on the throne, hoping to create a Catholic, French and Spanish superstate. The Protestant nations opposed him, supporting the Austrian claimant.

1701 ~ Jethro Tull invents the seed drill

THE REIGN OF ANNE (1702–14)

1703 ~ St Petersburg founded by Peter the Great

1704 ~ Gibraltar captured

1704 ~ The Battle of Blenheim, the Duke of Marlborough thwarts Louis XIV's hopes of dominating Europe

1706 ~ The Battle of Ramillies, Marlborough conquers the Spanish Netherlands

1707 ~ The Act of Union, unites England and Scotland in the Kingdom of Great Britain:

> *'There's an end to ane old song.'*
> THE LORD CHANCELLOR OF SCOTLAND ON SIGNING THE ACT OF UNION

1708 ~ The Battle of Oudenarde, the British take Sardinia and Minorca

The charge of Marlborough's horse at the Battle of Blenheim.

1709 TO 1714

18th Century

1709 ~ The Battle of Malplaquet, victory over the French

1709 ~ Abraham Darby develops the blast furnace using coke

1710 ~ Christopher Wren's St Paul's Cathedral completed

1712 ~ Thomas Newcomen develops the piston engine

1713 ~ The Treaty of Utrecht ends the War of Spanish Succession

St Paul's Cathedral in 1710. Sir Christopher Wren, who designed it, was buried there in 1723.

THE HOUSE OF HANOVER
THE REIGN OF GEORGE I
(1714–27)

Having no immediate heir, Queen Anne and Parliament were forced to choose a successor towards the end of her life, and offered the throne to a granddaughter of James I, the Protestant Electress Sophia of Hanover in Germany.

But Sophia died before Anne, so it was her son, George, who became George I of England. George's very German-ness and tendency to spend as much time as possible in Hanover, led to the royal practice of leaving the Crown's interests in the hands of a trusted politician, the First or Prime Minister, who was in the first instance the Whig, Sir Robert Walpole, as George was suspicious of the Tories' Jacobite sympathies.

1714 ~ Jethro Tull develops his horse-drawn hoe

1714 ~ Gabriel Fahrenheit makes the first mercury thermometer

1715 ~ The First Jacobite Rebellion rises in support of The Old Pretender, James Edward Stuart, the son of James II and the father of Bonnie Prince Charlie

1715 ~ The Battle of Sheriffmuir, the Scottish Jacobites defeated

1715 ~ The death of Louis XIV of France

1715 ~ The Battle of Preston, the English Jacobites defeated

Louis XIV, The Sun King of France, who, on learning of Marlborough's victory at Blenheim said, 'How could God do this to me after all I have done for him?'.

1719 ~ Daniel Defoe's *Robinson Crusoe*

1720 ~ The Collapse of the South Sea Bubble:

'An undertaking of great advantage, but nobody to know what it is.'
COMPANY PROSPECTUS OF THE SOUTH SEA BUBBLE

The South Sea Company was set up to trade with South America and to provide funds for the government. Its scheme to take over part of the government debt led to hysterical speculation in its shares, and others, until the bubble burst, ruining many.

1721 ~ Sir Robert Walpole becomes First or 'Prime' Minister

'All those men have their price.'
OF HIS FELLOW PARLIAMENTARIANS

1725 ~ Jonathan Swift's *Gulliver's Travels*

1725 ~ Vivaldi's *The Four Seasons*

THE REIGN OF GEORGE II
(1727–60)

18th Century

1729 ~ John Wesley founds the Methodist Society:

1729 ~ JS Bach's *St Matthew Passion*

'I felt my heart strangely warmed. I felt I did trust in Christ, Christ alone for Salvation; and an assurance was given me that He had taken away my sins, even mine, and saved me from the Law of sin and death.'

1733 ~ John Kay patents faster shuttle looms

1735 ~ William Hogarth's *The Rake's Progress*

1739 ~ The War of Jenkins's Ear

1740–8 ~ The War of Austrian Succession

1740 ~ Samuel Richardson's *Pamela*

John Wesley's open air preaching touched thousands. He opened the first Methodist Chapel in Bristol in 1738.

18th Century

1741 ~ Frederick the Great beats the Austrians

1742 ~ George Frederic Handel's *Messiah*

1743 ~ The Battle of Dettingen, victory over the French. The last time an English King led his troops into battle

1744 ~ The first officially recorded modern cricket match

1745 ~ The Second Jacobite rebellion under 'Bonnie' Prince Charlie, grandson of James II

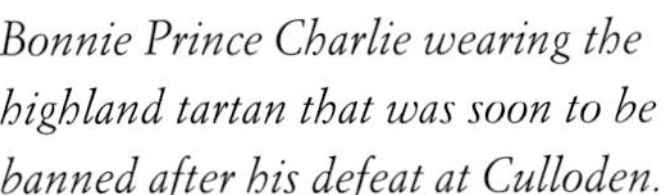

Bonnie Prince Charlie wearing the highland tartan that was soon to be banned after his defeat at Culloden.

1746 ~ The Battle of Culloden, the Jacobites defeated

1748 ~ William Cullen demonstrates refrigeration

1748 ~ David Hume's *An Enquiry Concerning Human Understanding*:

'Custom, then, is the great guide of human life...'

1749 ~ Henry Fielding's *Tom Jones*:

'When I mention religion, I mean the Christian religion; and not only the Christian religion, but the Protestant religion; and not only the Protestant religion but the Church of England.'

1753 TO 1757

18th Century

1753–1813 ~ The life of George Culley, the great sheep breeder

1754 ~ Josiah Wedgwood sets up his first pottery

1755 ~ *Dr Johnson's Dictionary*:

1755 ~ The Lisbon Earthquake

'Lexicographer: A writer of dictionaries. A harmless drudge.'

1756 ~ The Black Hole of Calcutta

Like the French and Portuguese traders in India, the British East India Company was forced to take sides in local politics or abandon their investments. The French and English East India Companies each had their own armies, which increasingly came into conflict. The Nawab of Bengal, supported by the French, captured the British East India Company's Fort William and confined 146 British prisoners in a cell 18ft by 14ft 10in. Only 22 men and one woman survived.

1756–63 ~ The Seven Years War. After some initial defeats in Europe, Britain ejected France from Canada and India

1756–1836 ~ The life of John McAdam who mixed tar and gravel to create tarmac

George II, the last English King to lead his troops into battle. He advanced on foot at the head of the infantry and defeated the French.

1757–1834 ~ The life of Thomas Telford, builder of the London to Holyhead road and the Menai Bridge

1757 TO 1765

18th Century

1757 ~ Robert Clive wins the Battle of Plassey:

'A great prince was dependent on my pleasure, an opulent city lay at my mercy; its richest bankers bid against each other for my smiles; I walked through vaults which were thrown open to me alone, piled on either hand with gold and jewels! Mr Chairman, at this moment I stand astonished at my own moderation.'

1759 ~ James Wolfe captures Quebec:

'Now God be praised, I will die in peace.'

HIS LAST WORDS, HAVING LEARNT OF HIS VICTORY

THE REIGN OF GEORGE III

FARMER GEORGE

(1760–1820)

'Born and educated in this country, I glory in the name of Briton.'

KING GEORGE

1761 ~ The Bridgwater Canal opened:

'Perhaps the greatest artificial curiosity in the world.'

1761 ~ 150 stockbrokers form a club at Jonathon's Coffee House to buy and sell shares

1763 ~ The Peace of Paris, which ends the Seven Years' War, grants Britain India and Canada

1764 ~ The Spinning Jenny invented by James Hargreaves

1765 ~ Colonial Stamp Duty

1766 TO 1775

18th Century

1766–8 ~ William Pitt the Elder, the Great Commoner, Prime Minister:

'The poorest man may in his cottage bid defiance to all the forces of the Crown.'

1767–76 ~ The Royal Crescent in Bath built

1768 ~ Sir Joshua Reynolds becomes the first President of the Royal Academy

1769 ~ James Watt's steam engine:

'I sell here, Sir, what all the world desires to have – power!'
MATTHEW BOULTON OF THE WATT BOULTON STEAM FACTORY

1770 ~ Thomas Gainsborough's *The Blue Boy*
1770 ~ Botany Bay discovered by Captain James Cook

1772 ~ Lord Mansfield's Judgement makes slavery illegal in England

1773 ~ The Stockbrokers' Club builds New Jonathon's in Sweeting Alley with a dealing room. It soon becomes known as The Stock Exchange

1773 ~ The Boston Tea Party in America

1775 ~ The First Maratha War
1775 ~ The Rotary action engine adopted by Arkwright

The Yorkshireman Captain Cook, in Whitby, whose prevention of scurvy through the use of lime juice was adopted by the Royal Navy.

Colonists take on the forces of the King on Lexington Common. Pitt the Elder said 'You cannot conquer America.'

1775–81 ~ The War of American Independence

1776 ~ The American Declaration of Independence:

'We hold these truths to be self evident, that all men are created equal: That they are endowed by their Creator with certain unalienable rights; that among these are life, liberty, and the pursuit of happiness.'

1776 ~ Edward Gibbon's *The Decline and Fall of the Roman Empire*
1776 ~ Adam Smith's *An Enquiry into the Nature and Causes of the Wealth of Nation*s:

'It is not from the benevolence of the butcher, the brewer, or the baker, that we expect our dinner, but from their regard to their own interest. We address ourselves not to their humanity but to their self love.'

18th Century

The 'centenary eruption' of Vesuvius, which occurred exactly one thousand seven hundred years after the disaster which destroyed Pompeii.

Britain	Abroad
	1779 ~ Vesuvius erupts
1780 ~ The first Derby	
1781 ~ The British surrender at Yorktown in America	
1782–1820 ~ The first Highland Clearances	
1783–1801 ~ William Pitt the Younger, Tory Prime Minister	**1783** ~ The Montgolfier brothers fly their hot air balloon in France
1783 ~ The death of Lancelot 'Capability' Brown	
1784 ~ Henry Cort puddles iron	
1785 ~ The first power loom invented by Edmund Cartwright	
1786 ~ The impeachment of the Indian Governor-General Warren Hastings	**1786** ~ Mozart's *The Marriage of Figaro*

1787 ~ The Kingdom of Ireland granted autonomy

1788 ~ A penal colony established at Botany Bay

Portrait of George Washington, who said there was 'something charming in the sound of whistling bullets'.

1789 ~ George Washington becomes the first President of the USA
1789 ~ The French Revolution

1790 ~ Edmund Burke's *Reflections on the French Revolution*:

'A state without the means of some change is without the means of its conservation.'
'It is necessary only for the good man to do nothing for evil to triumph.'

1792 ~ The Year of Canal Mania, 40 new canals projected, leading to 4,000 miles of inland waterways
1793–1802 ~ War with France

1795 ~ The Speenhamland Poor Relief System, which makes up wages to a basic minimum, is widely adopted in the south of England

Britain	Abroad
1796 ~ Vaccination against smallpox	**1796** ~ Napoleon Bonaparte's Italian Campaign

1796 TO 1802

18th ~ 19th Century

1798 ~ Insurrection of the United Irishmen

1798 ~ The Battle of the Nile, Horatio Nelson destroys the French fleet, stranding Napoleon in Egypt:

'Silence!
Cast loose your guns!
Level your guns!
Out tompions!
Prime!
Run out your guns!
Point your guns!
FIRE!'

1798 ~ Thomas Malthus's *Essay on the Principle of Population*

1798 ~ Income Tax introduced

1798 ~ Haydn's *The Creation*

1800 ~ Josiah Spode invents bone china which looks like porcelain but is cheaper and stronger

1800 ~ Italian physicist Alessandro Volta invents the electric battery

1801 ~ The General Enclosure Act, simplifies still further the enclosure of open fields and wasteland

1801 ~ The Act of Union creates the United Kingdom of Great Britain and Ireland

1801 ~ Nelson destroys the Danish fleet at Copenhagen

1802–03 ~ The Second Maratha War

The memorial bust of Nelson at Burnham Thorpe in his home county of Norfolk, showing his empty right sleeve, his arm having been shattered at Tenerife in 1797.

NELSON CENTENARY 1905
ERECTED BY THE LONDON SOCIETY OF EAST ANGLIANS IN MEMORY
OF ONE OF EAST ANGLIA'S MOST ILLUSTRIOUS AND HEROIC SONS
VICE ADMIRAL HORATIO VISCOUNT NELSON K.B. DUKE OF BRONTE

1803 TO 1805

19th Century

1803–15 ~ War with France

1803 ~ The Battle of Assaye, Wellington crushes the Marathas

1804–6 ~ William Pitt, the Younger, Tory Prime Minister:

'England has saved herself by her exertions, and will, as I trust, save Europe by her example.'

1804–6 ~ Parliamentary 'Coalition of all the talents'

1804 ~ Richard Trevithick invents his self-propelled engine

1805 ~ William Wordsworth's *Prelude*

1804 ~ Ludwig van Beethoven's *Eroica* Symphony

1804 ~ Napoleon crowns himself Emperor

Napoleon, who dismissed England as a nation of shopkeepers.

1805 ~ The Battle of Trafalgar:

'England expects that every man will do his duty.'
Horatio Nelson

'Kiss me Hardy.'
Nelson's last words

A detail from Nelson's Column, whose height matches that of the main mast of his flag ship, The Victory.

1805 ~ Napoleon defeats the Russian and Austrian armies at the Battle of Austerlitz (the Battle of the Three Emperors)

1807 ~ The Abolition of the slave trade

1808–14 ~ The Peninsular War

1808–32 ~ Goethe's *Faust*

1811 ~ The Luddites attack machinery

1811–20 ~ The Regency: George, Prince of Wales, Regent during the King's illness

1812–14 ~ War with the United States of America

1812 ~ Napoleon's army retreats from Moscow

1813 ~ Jane Austen's *Pride and Prejudice*:

1813 ~ Napoleon beaten at the Battle of Leipzig (the Battle of the Nations)

'It is a truth universally acknowledged, that a single man in possession of a good fortune, must be in want of a wife.'

19th Century

Wellington greets Blucher, the Commander of the Prussian Forces, who arrived on the field of Waterloo at the moment of victory.

1815 ~ The Battle of Waterloo:

'Ours is composed of the scum of the earth – the mere scum of the earth.'

THE DUKE OF WELLINGTON ON HIS ARMY

'Up guards and at 'em!'

THE DUKE OF WELLINGTON AT WATERLOO

1814 ~ Napoleon in exile on the Island of Elba

1815 ~ Napoleon escapes, returning to France

1815 ~ Brazil declares independence from Portugal

'Next to a battle lost, the greatest misery is a battle gained.'

THE DUKE OF WELLINGTON AFTER THE BATTLE OF WATERLOO

19th Century

1815 ~ Sir Humphry Davy invents his mining Safety Lamp

1815 ~ The Corn Law, forbidding the purchase of wheat from abroad until the price in Britain had reached 80 shillings a quarter, inflating the price of bread

1817 ~ Elizabeth Fry forms her Prison Improvement Association:

'Punishment is not for revenge but to reduce crime and reform the criminal.'

1818 ~ Chile declares independence from Spain

1819 ~ The Peterloo Massacre

A huge meeting of people from all over north-west England was held in St Peter's Fields in Manchester to demand reform. When the unarmed crowd was sabre-charged by the Yeoman Cavalry, 11 were killed, and 400 wounded.

1819–24 ~ Lord Byron's *Don Juan*:

'And after all what is a lie? Tis but
The truth in masquerade.'

THE REIGN OF GEORGE IV
(1820–30)

1820 ~ John Keats's *Ode to Autumn*:

'Season of mists and mellow fruitfullness,
close bosom friend of the maturing sun.'

An early Trade Union certificate, from the Amalgamated Society of Woodworkers.

Britain

1820 ~ The Cato Street conspiracy, fails to assassinate the Cabinet

1821 ~ John Constable's *The Hay Wain*

1822 ~ The death of Castlereagh

1823 ~ The first Rugby Football match

1825 ~ Trade Unions legalized
1825 ~ The Stockton and Darlington Railway opens, the first public steam railway

1829 ~ Catholic Emancipation

1829 ~ Sir Robert Peel creates the civilian Metropolitan Police Force, its men unarmed and dressed in blue to distinguish them from the army

1829 ~ Robert Stephenson demonstrates his steam locomotive, The Rocket

Abroad

1821 ~ Peru declares independence from Spain

1828 ~ The death of the Austrian composer, Franz Schubert

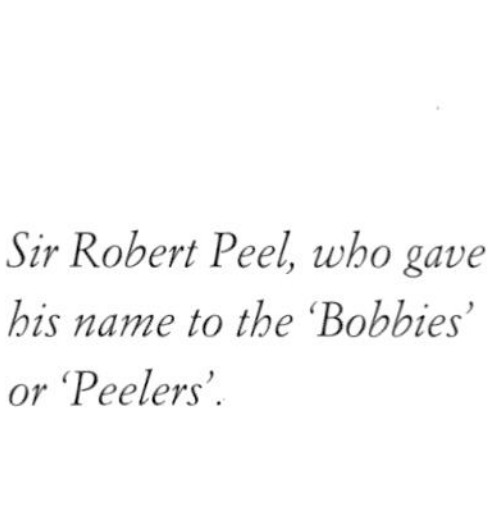
Sir Robert Peel, who gave his name to the 'Bobbies' or 'Peelers'.

The Reign of William IV, The Sailor King (1830–37)

1830 ~ The Liverpool and Manchester Railway opens

1830 ~ The July Revolution in France against Bourbon King Charles X

William IV, before he succeeded his brother, George IV. From 1790 to 1811 he lived happily with the actress Mrs Jordon, who bore him ten children.

1830s ~ Charles Babbage designs his Analytical Engine

1831 ~ Michael Faraday discovers electrical induction

1831 ~ James Ross reaches magnetic North

1832 ~ The Great Reform Bill, largely doing away with 'Rotten and Pocket Boroughs', and extending the vote by 50 per cent in England and Wales

1830 ~ The death of Venezuelan revolutionary leader Simón Bolívar whose victories won independence for Bolivia, Panama, Colombia, Ecuador, Peru and Venezuela

1831 ~ Belgium independent

1832 ~ Greece declares independence from the Ottoman Empire

1833 ~ The Factory Act bans the employment of children under nine
1833 ~ The Oxford Movement launched
1833 ~ Slavery abolished in the British Empire

1834 ~ The 'Tolpuddle Martyrs' sentenced to transportation for involvement in an early Union. All six pardoned in 1836 after public outcry

1835 ~ American inventor Samuel Colt designs the revolver

1836 ~ Charles Dickens's *The Pickwick Papers*:

*'It's always best on these occasions to do what the mob do.'
'But suppose there are two mobs?' suggested Mr Snodgrass.
'Shout with the largest,' replied Mr Pickwick.*

Charles Dickens, all of whose novels, except A Christmas Carol, *were published in instalments.*

1836 ~ The launch of the Chartist movement, calling for the secret ballot, fair electoral boundaries and the vote for working people

1836 ~ The South African Boers set out on the Great Trek to escape British rule
1836 ~ At the Siege of the Alamo, Texan rebels make a stand against Mexican rule

THE REIGN OF QUEEN VICTORIA, GRANDMOTHER OF EUROPE (1837–1901)

'I will be good.'

VICTORIA ON BEING SHOWN THE LINE OF SUCCESSION AS A CHILD

1837 ~ The first telegraphic message sent

1838 ~ Morse Code invented
1838 ~ The Anti-Corn Law League
1838–42 ~ The First Afghan War

1839 ~ Lord Durham's *Report on the Affairs of British North America*
1839 ~ The first Grand National
1839 ~ The bicycle invented in Scotland by Kirkpatrick MacMillan

1839–42 ~ The First Opium War, Britain gains Hong Kong

1840 ~ The first British Colonists arrive in New Zealand
1840 ~ The Penny Post
1840–54 ~ The Second Highland Clearances

1843 ~ Isambard Kingdom Brunel launches the first iron-hulled ship with a screw propeller, *The Great Britain*
1843 ~ Sir Charles Napier conquers Sind:

Queen Victoria and the Prince of Wales, the future Edward VII. Having nine children in all she seemed the archetype of Victorian motherhood.

'Peccavi!' (I have sinned)

1844 ~ JMW Turner's *Rain, Steam and Speed!*

1844 ~ The French defeat the Moroccans at the Battle of Isly in the Franco-Moroccan War

1845–6 ~ The Great Irish Potato Famine

1845–7 ~ Railway mania generates 576 new railway companies, with 18,700 miles of new track agreed

1846 ~ The Repeal of the Corn Laws

A family search for untainted potatoes. The Potato Blight is believed to have caused the death through starvation of one million in Ireland and Scotland.

1847 ~ William Thackeray's *Vanity Fair*

1848 ~ The end of the Chartist Movement

1849 ~ Victory over the Sikhs and the conquest of the Punjab

1847 ~ Liberia declares independence from the American Colonization Society

1848 ~ Marx and Engels's *Communist Manifesto*

1848 ~ In the Year of Revolutions, revolutions sweep through France, Italy, Germany, the Austrian Empire and Poland

1849 ~ The Californian Gold Rush

1850–65 ~ The Taiping Rebellion in China

1851 ~ Verdi's opera *Rigoletto*

Britain | Abroad

1851
TO
1855

19th Century

1851 ~ The Great Exhibition opens at the Crystal Palace:

'These, England's triumphs, are the trophies of a bloodless war.'
William Thackeray

1851 ~ Melville's *Moby Dick*

1852 ~ Napoleon III becomes Emperor of France

1853 ~ Sir George Cayley's coachman achieves the first manned glider flight

1854–6 ~ The Crimean War

Russia occupied parts of the Ottoman Empire in order to pressurize Turkey into allowing Orthodox priests to control the Holy Places in Jerusalem. The British and French Governments, fearing that Russia intended to expand into Eastern Europe, backed Turkey.

Melville sailed on a whaler in the South Seas and described it as 'his Yale College and Harvard'.

1854 ~ The Charge of the Light Brigade at Balaclava; the sick tended by Florence Nightingale, 'Lady of the Lamp':

'The very first requirement in a Hospital is that it should do the sick no harm!'

1855–8 ~ Henry Temple, Viscount Palmerston, Liberal Prime Minister:

'As the Roman, in days of old, held himself free from indignity, when he could say Civis Romanus sum*; so also a British Subject, in whatever land he may be, shall feel confident that the watchful eye and the strong arm of England will protect him against injustice and wrong.'*

1855 ~ Anthony Trollope's *The Warden*

Opposite: Queen Victoria was anxious that the exhibits in the Crystal Palace might be 'soiled by sparrows', and consulted the Duke of Wellington. His answer; 'Sparrowhawks Ma'am.'

19th Century

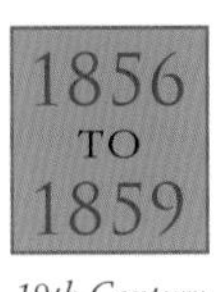

1856 TO 1859

19th Century

1856–60 ~ The Second Opium War, Britain and France force China to accept trade with Europe

1856 ~ Flaubert's *Madame Bovary*

1857 ~ Civil divorce becomes possible

1857–8 ~ The Indian Mutiny

By 1857 the East India Company ruled almost the whole of India and had its own private army. In 1857 some of the East India Company soldiers mutinied over the introduction of a new cartridge, rumoured to be smeared with pig fat (unclean to Muslims) and cow fat (sacred to Hindus). After hideous atrocities on both sides the mutiny was suppressed and the East India Company abolished in 1858.

Queen Victoria wrote in her diary of meeting her future husband (above) 'It was with some emotion that I beheld Albert – who is beautiful.'

1858 ~ Isambard Kingdom Brunel launches the *Great Eastern*, the largest ship in the world and the first with a double iron hull

1859 ~ John Stuart Mill's *On Liberty*:

'A state which dwarfs its men, in order that they be more docile instruments in its hands even for beneficial purposes, will find that with small men no great thing can really be accomplished.'

1859–65 ~ Henry Temple, Viscount Palmerston, Liberal Prime Minister

1859 ~ Charles Darwin's *The Origin of Species*:

'I have called this principle, by which each slight variation, if useful, is preserved, by the term of Natural Selection.'

1860 ~ Sir Charles Barry's Houses of Parliament open

1861 ~ The death of Prince Albert

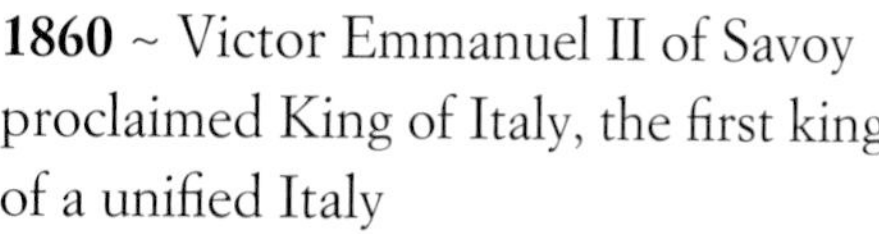

1860 ~ Victor Emmanuel II of Savoy proclaimed King of Italy, the first king of a unified Italy

1861 ~ Russian serfs liberated by Tsar Alexander II

1861–5 ~ The American Civil War, fought between the Unionist Northern states and the Confederate Southern states

A map of the battle of Antietam or Sharpsburg, the first battle of the Civil War on Northern soil and the bloodiest one-day battle in US history.

1862 TO 1868

19th Century

1862 ~ The American Dr Gatling makes the first machine gun, 'The Gatling gun'

1863 ~ The Football Association founded

1864 ~ Pasteurization invented by the French scientist Louis Pasteur
1864 ~ The International Red Cross founded in Switzerland

1864/5–70 ~ The War of the Triple Alliance (Paraguayan or López War)

1865 ~ American President Abraham Lincoln shot

Abraham Lincoln, US Republican President from 1861–5, who said, 'Those who deny freedom to others, deserve it not for themselves.'

1866 ~ Submarine telegraph cable laid across the Atlantic

1866 ~ Swedish scientist Alfred Nobel invents dynamite

1867 ~ Canada established as the first Dominion
1867 ~ Fenian insurrection in Ireland
1867 ~ The Second Reform Act gives the vote to 1 in 3 men

1867 ~ Karl Marx publishes *Das Kapital*

1868 ~ The first Trades Union Congress in Manchester

1868 ~ Punitive expedition to Ethiopia

1868–74 ~ William Gladstone, Liberal Prime Minister

William Gladstone, of whom Queen Victoria complained, 'He speaks to Me as if I was a public meeting.'

1868–9 ~ Robert Browning's *The Ring and The Book*

1869 ~ Diamonds discovered along the Vaal River in South Africa

1869 ~ The Suez Canal built, shortening the trade route between Europe and Asia

1870 ~ Forster's Education Act. Civil service exams

1870–1 ~ The Franco-Prussian War

1871 ~ The Paris Commune
1871–90 ~ Otto von Bismarck becomes the first Chancellor of the newly united Germany

1872 ~ Henry Stanley finds David Livingstone:

'Dr Livingstone, I presume?'

1872 ~ George Eliot publishes her novel *Middlemarch*

1872 ~ Leo Tolstoy's *Anna Karenina*

19th Century

Britain

1874–80 ~ Benjamin Disraeli, Conservative Prime Minister:

'There are three kinds of lies: lies, damned lies and statistics.'

1874 ~ Thomas Hardy's *Far from the Madding Crowd*

1875 ~ Suez Canal shares acquired
1875 ~ Gilbert and Sullivan's first operetta, *Trial by Jury*

1877 ~ Queen Victoria proclaimed Empress of India

Abroad

1874 ~ Remington No. 1, the first commercial typewriter
1874 ~ The first Impressionist exhibition held in Paris
1874 ~ Richard Wagner's operatic cycle *The Ring of the Niebelung* (the Ring Cycle)

1876 ~ Scottish scientist Alexander Graham Bell invents the telephone

India on the Albert Memorial in London. After her husband's death from Typhoid, the Queen was literally stunned with grief.

1878 ~ William Booth's Christian movement adopts the name The Salvation Army

19th Century

1879 ~ The Zulu War

1879 ~ American inventor Thomas Edison demonstrates his electric light bulb

1880 ~ The Education Act makes school compulsory for children aged 5–10

1880–1 ~ The First Boer War, Boer settlers in the Transvaal revolt against British rule

1880–5 ~ William Gladstone, Liberal Prime Minister:

'Money should fructify (bear fruit) in the pockets of the people.'

1880 ~ WG Grace scores the first ever test century against Australia

The Zulu impis of King Shaka wiped out a British army column at Isandhlwana.

1881–4 ~ Jewish pogroms in Imperial Russia

1882 ~ The occupation of Egypt

1882 ~ German engineer Daimler invents the petrol engine

1883 ~ Krakatoa Volcano erupts in Indonesia

1885 ~ General Gordon killed at Khartoum

1885 ~ The Third Reform Act

1885 ~ German engineer Karl Benz builds the first petrol-fuelled car

1886 ~ Gold discovered in the Transvaal

1886 ~ Coca-Cola concocted by American pharmacist John Pemberton

19th Century

1886 ~ Burma conquered

1886 ~ First Irish Home Rule Bill defeated

1887 ~ China's Yellow River floods, killing one million

1888 ~ Rudyard Kipling's *Plain Tales from the Hills*

1888 ~ Vincent van Gogh's *Sunflowers*

1889 ~ Cecil Rhodes establishes the British South Africa Company:

'Remember that you are an Englishman, and have consequently won first prize in the lottery of life.'

1893 ~ Second Irish Home Rule Bill rejected by Lords

1893 ~ Women given the vote in New Zealand

1894 ~ Captain Alfred Dreyfus convicted of treason by a French court-martial

'Marconigrams', named after their inventor Guglielmo Marconi, were messages transmitted without wires. They were initially regarded as so incredible that they had to be seen to be believed.

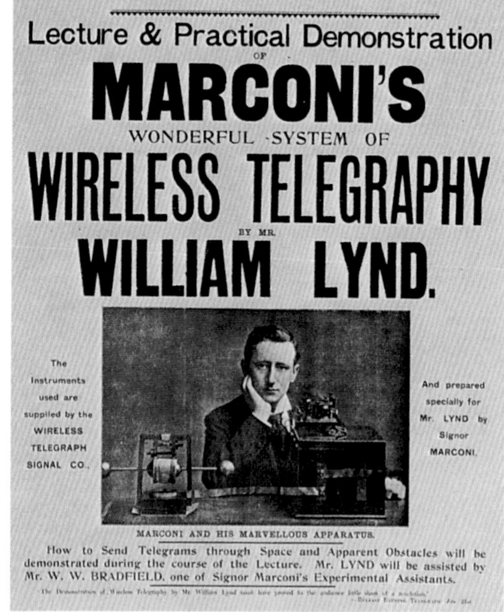

1895 ~ The Jameson Raid fails to spark a revolt by British settlers in the Transvaal

1895 ~ The trial of Oscar Wilde

1895 ~ Marconi transmits the first wireless message

1896 ~ The Klondike Gold Rush in Canada

1896 ~ The first modern Olympic Games held in Athens

Britain

1896 ~ The *Daily Mail* launched
1896 ~ The conquest of Sudan
1896 ~ The first cinema opens in Leicester Square, London

1898 ~ The Battle of Omdurman, the Khalifa's Army destroyed in Sudan

1899 ~ Edward Elgar's *Enigma Variations*

1899–1902 ~ The Second Boer War

Anticipating a British invasion after the Jameson Raid, the Boers declared war in October. British weight of numbers eventually overwhelmed the Boers but not before all Boer towns had been taken and the population 'concentrated' into camps to stop them assisting their guerrilla commandos.

> *'We are not interested in the possibilities of defeat; they do not exist.'*
> Queen Victoria

Abroad

1898 ~ America wins the Spanish-American War, gaining the Spanish colonies of Cuba, the Philippines, Guam and Puerto Rica

1898 ~ Radium discovered by the French scientists Pierre and Marie Curie

Queen Victoria visits British soldiers wounded in the Boer War, though disease also took a terrible toll.

1900
TO
1901

20th Century

1900 ~ The Labour Party founded:

'To secure for the workers by hand or by brain the full fruits of their industry and the most equitable distribution thereof that may be possible upon the basis of the common ownership of the means of production, distribution and exchange.'

CLAUSE FOUR (1918)

1900 ~ The Boxer Rebellion in China

1901 ~ Australia becomes the first self-governing member of the British Empire

1901 ~ Austrian psychiatrist Sigmund Freud's *The Psychopathology of Everyday Life*

THE HOUSE OF SAXE-COBURG-GOTHA
THE REIGN OF EDWARD VII
(1901–10)

1902–5 ~ Arthur Balfour, Conservative Prime Minister:

'The tyranny of majorities may be as bad as the tyranny of kings.'

1904 ~ Anglo-French Entente Cordiale

1902 ~ Cuba declares independence from the USA

1903 ~ The American Wright brothers achieve the first manned, powered flight

1904–5 ~ The Russo-Japanese War

Opposite: Sir William Nicholson's portrait of Queen Victoria in 1899, still in black for Prince Albert 38 years after his death.

Japanese diplomats set sail for Europe and the US to discuss Japan's conflict with Russia.

1905–8 ~ Sir Henry Campbell-Bannerman, Liberal Prime Minister

1906 ~ The launch of HMS *Dreadnought*, making all other battleships obsolete and initiating the naval arms race

1905 ~ German physicist Albert Einstein's *Special Theory of Relativity*

1906 ~ The San Francisco earthquake

20th Century

Britain

1907 ~ The Triple Entente, Britain now clearly allied with Russia and France against the Triple Alliance of Germany, Austria-Hungary and Italy

1908 ~ Robert Baden-Powell founds the Boy Scout movement

Edward VII's remarkable charm convinced the French to make an alliance with Britain. His son George remembered him as 'the best of friends and the best of fathers'.

1908–16 ~ Herbert Henry Asquith, Liberal Prime Minister

'(The War Office kept three sets of figures:) one to mislead the public, another to mislead the cabinet, and a third to mislead itself.'

1908 ~ The Old Age Pensions Act

1909 ~ Employment exchanges introduced

1909 ~ Lloyd George's 'People's Budget' rejected by the House of Lords

1910 ~ Rudyard Kipling's *If*:

'If you can fill the unforgiving minute
With sixty seconds' worth of distance run,
Yours is the Earth and everything that's in it,
And – which is more – you'll be a Man, my son!'

Abroad

1907 ~ American chemist Leo Baekeland invents plastic

1907 ~ The Model T Ford goes into production

1910 ~ Japan occupies Korea

THE HOUSE OF WINDSOR
THE REIGN OF GEORGE V
(1910–36)

1911 ~ The Delhi Durbar

1911 ~ The first National Health Insurance Bill

1911 ~ The House of Lords' veto abolished

1912 ~ The sinking of the *Titanic*

1912 ~ Captain Robert Scott's last expedition, to the South Pole:

'I am just going outside and may be some time.'
Captain Oates

Captain Scott at the South Pole. 'Great God, this is an awful place!' he wrote in his diary.

1912 ~ The Passage of the Irish Home Rule Bill

1913–14 ~ Charlie Chaplin appears in his first film, *Making a Living*

1914 ~ The Panama Canal opens, connecting the Pacific and Atlantic oceans

THE GREAT WAR, THE FIRST WORLD WAR
(1914–18)

'Their name liveth for ever more.'
The Stone of Sacrifice

The heir to the Austrian throne, Archduke Ferdinand, was assassinated by a Serb in Sarajevo, provoking the Austrians, allied with Germany, into attacking the Serbs, supported by Russia.
In order to knock out France before it came to the aid of its ally Russia, Germany put the Schlieffen plan into action, attacking France through Belgium.
Britain honoured its alliance with Belgium by sending the 'Old Contemptibles', the small but highly professional British Expeditionary Force, which held up the Germans long enough for the French to come up from Paris.

1914 TO 1916

20th Century

Field Marshall Kitchener oversaw the voluntary enlistment of over 3,000,000 men, like these in Newcastle.

1914 ~ The British Expeditionary Force sent to defend Belgium

1914–18 ~ The British hold Ypres

1915 ~ Gallipoli, the Allied invasion of Turkey fails

1915 ~ Rupert Brooke's *The Soldier*:

1914 ~ Archduke Franz Ferdinand of Austria assassinated by a Serb in Sarajevo

1914 ~ The French face the Germans on the River Marne

1915–18 ~ Christian Armenians massacred in Turkey

1915 ~ Germans initiate the use of poison gas

'If I should die, think only this of me:
That there's some corner of a foreign field
That is forever England.'

1916–22 ~ David Lloyd George, Liberal Prime Minister

Britain

1916 ~ Conscription introduced
1916 ~ The Battle of the Somme
1916 ~ The Battle of Jutland, the Royal Navy forces the German Fleet back to port

1916 ~ The Easter Rising in Dublin

Lawrence of Arabia, who said, 'Dreamers of the day are dangerous men, for they may act their dreams with open eyes and make them possible.'

1917 ~ The Battle of Passchendaele

1917 ~ 'Lawrence of Arabia' leads the Arab revolt against the Turks
1917 ~ US troops arrive in France
1917 ~ The Russian Revolution

1918 ~ The German spring offensive defeated

1918 ~ US President Wilson's 14 points for peace include the principle of self-determination

1918 At 11am, on November 11, Armistice signed between the Allies and Germany, ending the Great War

'What is our task? To make Britain a fit country for Heroes to live in.'
David Lloyd George

1918 ~ The vote given to all men over 21, and women over 30

1918–22 ~ The Russian Civil War

1918–19 ~ The Spanish influenza pandemic kills 25–40 million

1919 ~ The Treaty of Versailles
1919 ~ Six of the nine counties of Ulster elect for partition from the Irish Free State

1919 ~ The League of Nations created

20th Century

Britain

1919–20 ~ The Anglo-Irish War, the Irish Republican Army (IRA) demands independence for the whole island of Ireland

1920 ~ Ulster secedes from Ireland

1921 ~ Ernest Rutherford and James Chadwick split the atom

1922–3 ~ Andrew Bonar Law, Conservative Prime Minister

1922 ~ TS Eliot's *The Wasteland*
1922 ~ James Joyce's *Ulysses*
1922 ~ The Anglo-Irish Treaty signed, confirming the Partition of Ireland

1922–3 ~ The Irish Civil War fought between those members of the IRA who supported the Anglo-Irish Treaty and those who opposed it

1923–4 ~ Stanley Baldwin, Conservative Prime Minister

1924 ~ Ramsay MacDonald, Labour Prime Minister

1924–9 ~ Stanley Baldwin, Conservative Prime Minister

1925 ~ Return to the Gold Standard

1926 ~ The General Strike
1926 ~ John Logie Baird invents television

Abroad

1920–33 ~ Prohibition (of alcohol) in the USA

1921 ~ Adolf Hitler becomes leader of Germany's Nazi party

1922 ~ Italian Fascist leader Benito Mussolini leads the March on Rome

1922–91 ~ The Union of Soviet Socialist Republics (USSR) or Soviet Union

1924 ~ The death of Lenin
1924 ~ Joseph Stalin takes power in the Soviet Union

1927
TO
1930

20th Century

Stalin, Soviet Dictator, who described a single death as a tragedy, but a million as a statistic.

1927 ~ American aviator Charles Lindbergh makes the first non–stop solo flight across the Atlantic Ocean

1927 ~ The first talking motion picture, *The Jazz Singer*

1928 ~ DH Lawrence's *Lady Chatterley's Lover*, and Evelyn Waugh's *Decline and Fall*

1928 ~ Sir Alexander Fleming discovers penicillin

1929 ~ Votes for women over 21
1929 ~ The BBC begins television broadcasting

1929 ~ The Wall Street Crash
1929 ~ Ernest Hemingway's *A Farewell to Arms*

1929–35 ~ Ramsay MacDonald, Labour Prime Minister

1930 ~ Mohandas (the Mahatma) Gandhi leads the Salt March in India

1931 TO 1936

20th Century

Britain

1931 ~ National Government led by Ramsay MacDonald

1931–2 ~ Three million out of work (22 per cent)
1931 ~ The British Dominions become independent

1931 ~ The Statute of Westminster brings the British Commonwealth of Nations into existence, originally consisting of the six self-governing Dominions of Canada, Newfoundland, Australia, New Zealand, South Africa and the Irish Free State

1931 ~ The Gold Standard abandoned

1935–7 ~ Stanley Baldwin, Conservative Prime Minister
1935 ~ Watson Watt devises radar

1936 ~ John Maynard Keynes's *General Theory of Employment, Interest and Money*

1936 ~ Edward VIII abdicates, choosing the American divorcée Mrs Wallis Simpson over the throne:

'Our cock won't fight.'
LORD BEAVERBROOK TO WINSTON CHURCHILL

Abroad

1931 ~ Japan invades Manchuria

1932–3 ~ Stalin's Farm Collectivization causes the death of millions in the Ukraine

1933 ~ Adolf Hitler becomes Chancellor of Germany

1936 ~ Italy annexes Abyssinia
1936 ~ Germany occupies the Rhineland, breaking the Treaty of Versailles

1936–9 ~ The Spanish Civil War

1936 ~ Pablo Picasso's *Guernica*

THE REIGN OF GEORGE VI
(1936–52)

'And I said to the man who stood at the gate of the year: "Give me a light that I may tread safely into the unknown." And he replied: "Go into the darkness and put your hand into the hand of God. That shall be to you better than a light and safer than a known way."'

King George quoting ML Haskins in his 1939 Christmas broadcast

1937 ~ Frank Whittle invents the jet engine

1937–40 ~ Neville Chamberlain, Conservative Prime Minister

1938 ~ Chamberlain negotiates with Hitler at Munich:

'I believe it is peace for our time.'

1937 ~ The Irish Free State becomes Eire

1938 ~ Nazi Germany annexes Austria

1939 ~ The Nazi-Soviet Pact

Adolf Hitler, who said that 'the broad mass of a nation will more easily fall victim to a big lie than to a small one.'

THE SECOND WORLD WAR

(1939–45)

'When you go home, tell them of us and say, for your tomorrow we gave our today.'

The Kohima War Memorial

1939 ~ Germany invades Poland

1939 ~ The Soviet Union invades Poland

1939–40 ~ The Soviet Union occupies the Baltic States and invades Finland

Winston Churchill, who said it was the British nation who had the lion's heart. He had the luck to give the roar.

1940–5 ~ Winston Churchill, Conservative Prime Minister:

'I have nothing to offer but blood, toil, tears and sweat.'

1940 ~ The Evacuation of Dunkirk, rescuing Allied forces trapped on the beaches with their backs to the sea:

'Let us therefore brace ourselves to our duties, and so bear ourselves that, if the British Empire and its Commonwealth last for a thousand years, men will still say, "This was their finest hour."'

Churchill

1940 ~ The Battle of Britain, the RAF wins the 'battle of the skies', forcing Hitler to put off invasion

1940 ~ Germany, Japan and Italy form the Axis

'Never in the field of human conflict was so much owed by so many to so few.'

Churchill

RAF Memorial Chapel, Biggin Hill, Kent. The spitfire and radar were crucial, but it was the airmen of the RAF who had to take on the Germans in the sky.

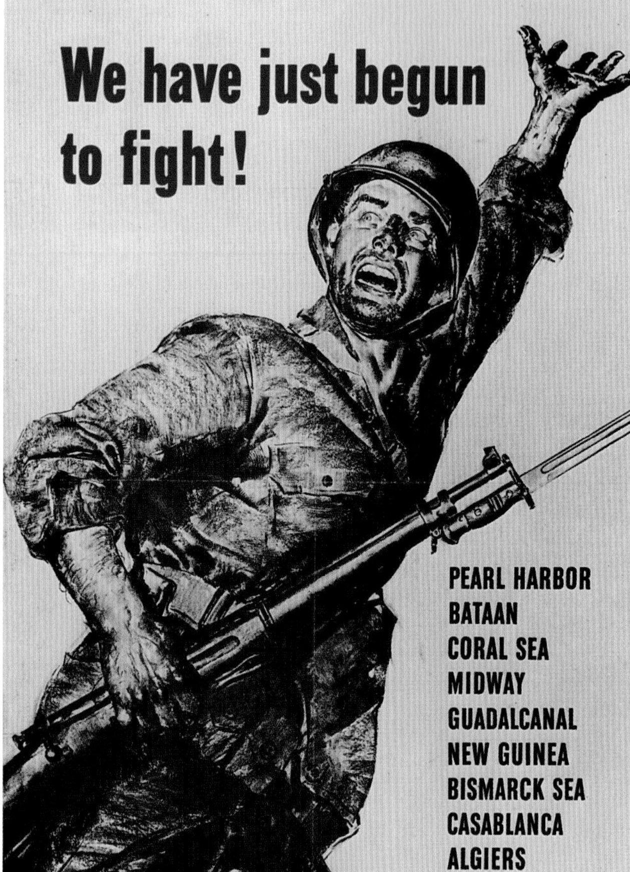

1940 ~ Walt Disney's animated film, *Fantasia*

1940 ~ German Blitzkrieg overwhelms Belgium, Holland and France

1940 ~ The first McDonald's restaurant opens in America

1941 ~ Hitler invades the Soviet Union
1941 ~ Pearl Harbor bombed

Opposite: Soldiers pray over a dead comrade in a stained glass window in Willingdon, Sussex.

In 1940 Democratic US President Franklin Roosevelt said America must be the 'arsenal of democracy'. After Pearl Harbour, the Americans were to use that arsenal themselves.

1942 ~ The Beveridge Report sets out a national insurance scheme designed to abolish the 'five giants' of want, disease, ignorance, squalor and idleness

1942 ~ The fall of Singapore to the Japanese
1942 ~ The Battle of El Alamein, the British Eighth Army drives the Germans out of Egypt

1943 ~ In the Battle of the Atlantic, German U-Boat packs sink 300 ships in the spring alone
1943 ~ The Allies invade Italy

1942 ~ The Wannsee Conference discusses 'The Jewish Question' and decides on 'The Final Solution', the extermination of all European Jews; the Holocaust

1943 ~ Germans surrender in North Africa and Stalingrad
1943 ~ Mussolini overthrown in Italy

1944 ~ The D-Day invasion of France
1944 ~ Butler's Education Act
1944 ~ At the Battle of Imphal, British and Indian troops defeat the Japanese

1944 ~ The Liberation of Paris

1945–51 ~ Clement Atlee, Labour Prime Minister, initiates Nationalization:

1945 ~ The Allied Yalta Conference
1945 ~ The United Nations established

'Democracy means government by discussion, but it is only effective if you can stop people talking.'

1945 ~ Unconditional surrender of all German forces in Europe on May 7

1945 ~ Atomic bombs dropped on Nagasaki and Hiroshima, leading to Japanese surrender on August 15

1946 ~ The National Health Service created

'An iron curtain has descended across the continent.'
CHURCHILL ON EUROPE

Chuck Yeager breaks the sound barrier flying at Mach I.

1948 ~ West Indian immigrants arrive on the SS *Empire Windrush*

1949 ~ George Orwell's *1984*:

'Who controls the past controls the future: who controls the present controls the past.'

1951–5 ~ Winston Churchill, Conservative Prime Minister

1951 ~ The Festival of Britain

1947 ~ The Americans break the speed of sound
1947 ~ India, Pakistan and Burma gain independence
1948 ~ The Jewish National Council declares the establishment of the new State of Israel
1949 ~ The Berlin Airlift relieves the Soviet blockade
1949 ~ The People's Republic of China established
1949 ~ Eire becomes the Irish Republic and leaves the Commonwealth
1949 ~ NATO (North Atlantic Treaty Organization) founded

1950–3 ~ The Korean War

Opposite: Shy and serious, with a stutter, Albert, Duke of York, never wanted or expected to be King, but as George VI he and his Queen led the nation that saved the world.

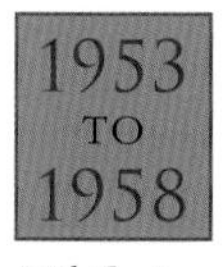

1953 TO 1958

20th Century

THE REIGN OF QUEEN ELIZABETH II
(1952–)

'I declare before you all that my whole life, whether it be long or short, shall be devoted to your service and the service of our great Imperial family to which we all belong.'

The Queen

1953 ~ Francis Crick and James Watson identify the structure of DNA

1953 ~ The death of Stalin

1954 ~ JRR Tolkien's *The Lord of the Rings*

1954 ~ The USA rules educational segregation unconstitutional

1954 ~ Rationing ends

1954–62 ~ The Algerian War of Independence

1955–7 ~ Sir Anthony Eden, Conservative Prime Minister:

'Long experience has taught me that to be criticized is not always to be wrong.'

1955–72 ~ The First Sudanese Civil War

1956 ~ The Suez Crisis, France, Britain and Israel attack Egypt after President Nasser closes the Suez Canal, but are forced by the USA to back down

1956 ~ Soviet invasion of Hungary

1956 ~ John Osborne's play *Look Back in Anger*

1956 ~ Nuclear power station Calder Hall opens

1957 ~ Ghana gains independence

1957 ~ The Treaty of Rome creates the European Economic Community (EEC)

1957–63 ~ Harold Macmillan, Conservative Prime Minister:

'Let us be frank about it: most of our people have never had it so good.'

1958 ~ Empire Day, the second Monday in March, becomes Commonwealth Day

1958 ~ General Charles de Gaulle made President of France

Britain  Abroad

1959 ~ First motorway, the M1, opens

1958 ~ Chairman Mao Tse-Tung's Great Leap Forward leads to widespread famine and the death of 20–30 million Chinese

'The wind of change is blowing through the continent.'
HAROLD MACMILLAN ON AFRICA, 1960

1960 ~ National Service ends

1961 ~ The Contraceptive Pill becomes available

1960 ~ The Sino-Soviet rift between Chinese and Russian Communists

1960 ~ Nigeria gains independence

1961 ~ Russian Yuri Gagarin becomes the first man in space

Her Majesty Queen Elizabeth II, who, since 1952, has 'reigned with our loves'.

'Groups with guitars are on the way out', the Beatles were told by Decca in 1961. It was only a year later that 'Please Please Me' reached No. 1.

Britain	Abroad
1962 ~ The Beatles reach No. 1	**1962** ~ The Cuban Missile Crisis
1963–4 ~ Sir Alec Douglas-Home, Conservative Prime Minister	**1963** ~ American President John F Kennedy shot **1963–75** ~ The Vietnam War
1964–70 ~ Harold Wilson, Labour Prime Minister:	

'The Britain that is going to be forged in the White Heat of this revolution will be no place for restrictive practices or for outdated methods on either side of industry.'

20th Century

Britain

1965 ~ Rhodesia makes the Unilateral Declaration of Independence (UDI)

1965 ~ Capital punishment abandoned

1966 ~ England wins the World Cup

1967 ~ Homosexual acts and abortion legalized

1968 ~ Civil 'Troubles' begin in Northern Ireland

1969 ~ Indians forced out of Uganda and Kenya flee to Britain

1969 ~ North Sea oil discovered

Abroad

1966 ~ The Cultural Revolution enforced in China

1967 ~ The Six Day War between Israel and Egypt

1968 ~ The Russian invasion of Czechoslovakia

1969 ~ American astronaut Neil Armstrong becomes the first man on the moon

The Archbishop of Canterbury said the landing on the moon made him even more proud of his humanity.

BRITISH | ABROAD

20th Century

1969 ~ Voting age lowered from 21 to 18

1969 ~ The Divorce Act becomes effective

1970–4 ~ Edward Heath, Conservative Prime Minister

1971 ~ Decimal coinage introduced

1972 ~ Bloody Sunday. Devolved government in Northern Ireland suspended

1973 ~ The UK joins the European Common Market

1973 ~ The Americans leave Vietnam

1973 ~ The Yom Kippur War

1974–6 ~ Harold Wilson, Labour Prime Minister

1975 ~ The Equal Opportunities Act

1975–9 ~ The Khmer Rouge kill 1.7 million in Cambodia

1976 ~ Concorde enters service

1976–9 ~ Jim Callaghan, Labour Prime Minister:

'Crisis? What Crisis?'

1977 ~ The Queen celebrates her Silver Jubilee:

'In times when nothing stood
but worsened, or grew strange
there was one constant good:
SHE did not change.'

PHILIP LARKIN

1979 ~ Failed British Referenda on Devolution for Wales and Scotland

1979 ~ The Shah of Iran overthrown

Margaret Thatcher, dubbed The Iron Lady by the Soviet Red Star, and described by President Mitterrand as having the eyes of Caligula and the lips of Marilyn Monroe.

1979 ~ The Winter of Discontent

1979–90 ~ Margaret Thatcher, Conservative Prime Minister, initiates privatization:

'Pennies don't fall from Heaven. They have to be earned on Earth.'

1979 ~ Ronald Reagan elected President of the USA

1979–92 ~ War in Afghanistan

20th Century

Britain

1980 ~ Majority rule in Rhodesia

1982 ~ The Falklands War

1984 ~ The Miners' Strike
1984 ~ The IRA Brighton Bomb

'This was the day I was meant not to see.'
MARGARET THATCHER

1986 ~ The Single European Act

1990 ~ John Major, Conservative Prime Minister

Abroad

1980–8 ~ The Iran–Iraq War

1985 ~ Mikhail Gorbachev comes to power in USSR

1986 ~ The USA bombs Libya in retaliation for the Libyan bombing of a Berlin nightclub

1989 ~ Solidarity takes power in Poland
1989 ~ The Tiananmen Square Massacre
1989 ~ The Berlin Wall torn down

1990 ~ Iraq invades and occupies Kuwait

US and coalition Air Force aeroplanes embark on Desert Storm.

Britain | Abroad

20th ~ 21st Century

1991 ~ Britain signs the Maastricht Treaty

1991 ~ The First Gulf War

1991 ~ Sir Tim Berners Lee invents the World Wide Web

1991 ~ Boris Yeltsin defies coup against the Soviet Premier Gorbachev

1991 ~ The Soviet Union dissolved

1991–5 ~ Civil Wars in the former Yugoslavia

1992 ~ Britain leaves the European Exchange Rate Mechanism

1993 ~ Civil War breaks out in the Sudan

1994 ~ Hutus slaughter 900,000 in Rwanda

1994 ~ Apartheid ends in South Africa

1996 ~ Dolly the sheep cloned in Scotland

1996–7 ~ The First Congo Civil War

1997– ~ Tony Blair, Labour Prime Minister:

1997 ~ Hong Kong surrendered to the People's Republic of China

'I'm a straight kinda guy.'

1997 ~ The death of Diana, Princess of Wales

1998 ~ The Good Friday Agreement

1998–2003 ~ The Second Congo Civil War, nearly 4 million die of starvation and disease

1999 ~ Devolution for Wales and Scotland

1999 ~ The Euro currency launched

2000 ~ The (1998) Human Rights Act becomes effective, the European Convention on Human Rights is incorporated into British Law

2000 ~ Concorde crashes in Paris

2001 ~ The Foot and Mouth crisis, 6.5 million animals needlessly slaughtered

2001 ~ Nine Eleven, Al Qaeda hijackers fly two aeroplanes into the twin towers of the World Trade Center in New York

21st Century

2002 ~ The British army restores order in Sierra Leone

2002 ~ The Countryside March in London in support of hunting with hounds. The largest demonstration in British history

2003 ~ The Second Gulf War liberates Iraq from Saddam Hussein

2003 ~ England wins the Rugby World Cup

2005 ~ Hunting with hounds banned

2005 ~ Hereditary peers purged from the House of Lords

2005 ~ England wins the Ashes

2005 ~ The 7/7 public transport bombs explode in Central London:

2003 ~ Militia massacres in Darfur, western Sudan

2004 ~ The Boxing Day Tsunamis spread through the Indian Ocean, devastating the coasts of Indonesia, Sri Lanka, India and Thailand

2005 ~ Pope John Paul II dies in the Vatican

2005 ~ The Dutch and French electorates reject the proposed European Constitution

'Those who perpetrate these brutal acts against innocent people should know they will not change our way of life. Atrocities such as these simply reinforce our sense of community, our humanity, and our trust in the rule of Law.'

QUEEN ELIZABETH II

Commandments, Charters & Speeches

Preaching to the King at St Paul's Cross, London, 1635.

THE TEN COMMANDMENTS

Exodus 20: The King James Bible

And God spake all these words, saying, I am the Lord thy God, which have brought thee out of the land of Egypt, out of the house of bondage.

Thou shalt have no other gods before me.

Thou shalt not make unto thee any graven image, or any likeness of any thing that is in heaven above, or that is in the earth beneath, or that is in the water under the earth:

Thou shalt not bow down thyself to them, nor serve them: for I the Lord thy God am a jealous God, visiting the iniquity of the fathers upon the children unto the third and fourth generation of them that hate me; And shewing mercy unto thousands of them that love me, and keep my commandments.

Thou shalt not take the name of the Lord thy God in vain; for the Lord will not hold him guiltless that taketh his name in vain.

Remember the sabbath day, to keep it holy. Six days shalt thou labour, and do all thy work: But the seventh day is the sabbath of the Lord thy God: in it thou shalt not do any work, thou, nor thy son, nor thy daughter, thy manservant, nor thy maidservant, nor thy cattle, nor thy stranger that is within thy gates: For in six days the Lord made heaven and earth, the sea, and all that in them is, and rested the seventh day: wherefore the Lord blessed the sabbath day, and hallowed it.

Honour thy father and thy mother: that thy days may be long upon the land which the Lord thy God giveth thee.

Thou shalt not kill.

Thou shalt not commit adultery.

Thou shalt not steal.

Thou shalt not bear false witness against thy neighbour.

Thou shalt not covet thy neighbour's house, thou shalt not covet thy neighbour's wife, nor his manservant, nor his maidservant, nor his ox, nor his ass, nor any thing that is thy neighbour's.

JESUS

THE GREAT COMMANDMENT

Matthew 22: The King James Bible

Thou shalt love the Lord thy God with all thy heart, and with all thy soul, and with all thy mind.

This is the first and great Commandment.

And the second is like unto it, Thou shalt love thy neighbour as thyself.

On these two commandments hang all the law and the prophets.

JESUS
FROM THE SERMON ON THE MOUNT
MATTHEW 6, THE KING JAMES BIBLE

Jesus delivering The Sermon on the Mount, All Saints Church, Ledsham.

After this manner therefore pray ye:

OUR FATHER WHICH art in heaven,
Hallowed be thy name.
Thy kingdom come.
Thy will be done in earth,
as it is in heaven.
Give us this day our daily bread.
And forgive us our debts,
as we forgive our debtors.
And lead us not into temptation,
but deliver us from evil:
For thine is the kingdom,
and the power, and the glory, for ever. Amen.

THE SPEECH BY ONE OF KING EDWIN OF NORTHUMBRIA'S SAXON NOBLEMEN IN FAVOUR OF CHRISTIANITY
FROM THE *ECCLESIASTICAL HISTORY OF THE ENGLISH PEOPLE* BY THE VENERABLE BEDE

SUCH SEEMETH TO ME, my lord the present life of men here on earth…as if a sparrow should come to the house and very swiftly flit through…which entereth in at one window and straightaway passeth out through another while you sit at dinner with your captains and servants in wintertime; the parlour being then made warm with the fire kindled in the midst thereof, but all places being troubled with raging tempests of winter rain and snow. Right for the time it be within the house it feeleth no smart of the winter storm but after a very short space of fair weather it soon passeth again from winter to winter and escapeth your sight. So the life of man here appeareth for a little season, but what followeth or what hath gone before that surely we know not. Wherefore if this new learning hath brought us any better surety, methinks it is worthy to be followed.

THE MAGNA CARTA
THE GREAT CHARTER OF LIBERTIES
EXTORTED FROM KING JOHN BY HIS BARONS IN 1215

CLAUSE 39:

NO FREE MAN SHALL BE taken or imprisoned or dispossessed, or outlawed or exiled, or in any way destroyed, nor will we go upon him, nor will we send against him except by the lawful judgement of his peers or by the law of the land.

CLAUSE 40:

To no man will we sell, or deny, or delay, right or Justice.

ENGLAND
ACT II, SCENE I, RICHARD II
BY WILLIAM SHAKESPEARE

THIS ROYAL THRONE of kings, this scepter'd isle,
This earth of majesty, this seat of Mars,
This other Eden, demi-paradise,
This fortress built by Nature for herself
Against infection and the hand of war,
This happy breed of men, this little world,
This precious stone set in the silver sea,
Which serves it in the office of a wall,
Or as a moat defensive to a house,
Against the envy of less happier lands,
This blessed plot, this earth, this realm, this England,
This nurse, this teeming womb of royal kings,
Fear'd by their breed and famous by their birth,
Renowned for their deeds ... Far from home, -
For Christian service and true chivalry, -

Richard II as a boy with his grandfather, Edward III.

THE FEAST OF CRISPIAN
ACT IV, SCENE III, HENRY V
BY WILLIAM SHAKESPEARE

THIS DAY IS CALL'D the feast of Crispian:
He that outlives this day, and comes safe home,
Will stand a tip-toe when this day is nam'd,
And rouse him at the name of Crispian.
He that shall live this day, and see old age,
Will yearly on the vigil feast his neighbours,
And say, 'To-morrow is Saint Crispian':
Then will he strip his sleeve and show his scars,
And say, 'These wounds I had on Crispin's day'.
Old men forget: yet all shall be forgot,
But he'll remember with advantages
What feats he did that day. Then shall our names,
Familiar in his mouth as household words,
Harry the king, Bedford and Exeter,
Warwick and Talbot, Salisbury and Gloucester,
Be in their flowing cups freshly remember'd.
This story shall the good man teach his son;
And Crispin Crispian shall ne'er go by,
From this day to the ending of the world,
But we in it shall be remembered;
We few, we happy few, we band of brothers;
For he to-day that sheds his blood with me
Shall be my brother; be he ne'er so vile
This day shall gentle his condition:
And gentlemen in England, now a-bed
Shall think themselves accurs'd they were not here,
And hold their manhoods cheap whiles any speaks
That fought with us upon Saint Crispin's day.

ELIZABETH I

ADDRESSING HER TROOPS AT TILBURY WHILE AWAITING THE ARRIVAL OF THE SPANISH ARMADA IN 1588

MY LOVING PEOPLE, We have been persuaded by some that are careful of our safety to take heed how we commit ourselves to armed multitudes for fear of treachery, but I assure you I do not desire to live to distrust my faithful and loving people. Let Tyrants fear; I have always so behaved myself under God, I have placed my chiefest strength and safeguard in the loyal hearts and goodwill of my subjects. And therefore I am come amongst you, as you see, at this time not for my recreation and disport, but being resolved in the midst and heat of battle to live and die amongst you all. To lay down for God, my kingdom and for my people, my honour and my blood even in the dust. I know I have the body of a weak and feeble woman, but I have the heart and stomach of a King and a King of England too and think it foul scorn that Parma or Spain or any Prince of Europe should dare to invade the borders of my realm; to which, rather than any dishonour shall grow by me, I myself will take up arms, I myself will be your General, Judge and Rewarder of every one of your virtues in the field. I know already for your forwardness you have deserved rewards and crowns; and we do assure you, on the word of a Prince, they shall be duly paid you.

CHARLES I

FROM THE SCAFFOLD BEFORE HIS EXECUTION IN 1649

I NEVER DID BEGIN a War with the two Houses of Parliament, and I call God to witness, to whom I must shortly make an account, That I never did intend for to incroach upon their Privileges, they began upon me.

For the People … truly I desire their Liberty and Freedom as much as any body whomsoever; but I must tell you, That their Liberty and Freedom consist in having of Government, those Laws, by which their Life and their Goods may be most their own. It is not for having share in Government (Sir) that is nothing pertaining to them. A Subject and a Soveraign are clean different things.

I go from a corruptible to an incorruptible Crown; where no disturbance can be, no disturbance in the world.

SATAN

FROM PARADISE LOST BY JOHN MILTON

Satan rising from the burning lake in the first illustrated edition of Paradise Lost, *1688.*

WHAT THOUGH the field be lost?
All is not lost; the unconquerable Will,
And study of revenge, immortal hate,
And courage never to submit or yield:
And what is else not to be overcome?
That Glory never shall his wrath or might
Extort from me. To bow and sue for grace
With suppliant knee, and deifie his power
Who from the terrour of this Arm so late
Doubted his Empire, that were low indeed,
That were an ignominy and shame beneath
This downfall; since by Fate the strength of Gods
And this Empyreal substance cannot fail,
Since through experience of this great event
In Arms not worse, in foresight much advanc't,
We may with more successful hope resolve
To wage by force or guile eternal Warr
Irreconcileable, to our grand Foe,
Who now triumphs, and in th'excess of joy
Sole reigning holdst the Tyranny of Heav'n.

Charles I's religious convictions and sense of duty were too strong for him to compromise with his opponents.

WINSTON CHURCHILL

Speech in the House of Commons on 13th May 1940

I would say to the House, as I said to those who have joined this Government: 'I have nothing to offer but blood, toil, tears and sweat.' We have before us an ordeal of the most grievous kind. We have before us many, many long months of struggle and of suffering. You ask what is our policy? I will say: It is to wage war, by sea, land and air, with all our might and with all the strength that God can give us; to wage war against a monstrous tyranny, never surpassed in the dark, lamentable catalogue of human crime. That is our policy. You ask, What is our aim? I answer in one word: Victory – victory at all costs, victory in spite of all terror, victory, however long and hard the road may be; for without victory, there is no survival. Let that be realised; no survival for the British Empire; no survival for all that the British Empire has stood for, no survival for the urge and impulse of the ages, that mankind will move forward towards its goal. But I take up my task with buoyancy and hope. I feel sure that our cause will not be suffered to fail among men. At this time I feel entitled to claim the aid of all, and I say, 'Come, then, let us go forward together with our united strength.'

In order to invade Britain, 'Operation Sealion', and end the war, Hitler had to destroy the RAF. The Luftwaffe took on the RAF in the first proper air battle in history – and lost.

WINSTON CHURCHILL
Speech in the House of Commons on 4th June 1940

We shall not flag or fail. We shall go on to the end. We shall fight in France, we shall fight on the seas and oceans, we shall fight with growing confidence and growing strength in the air, we shall defend our island, whatever the cost may be. We shall fight on the beaches, we shall fight on the landing grounds, we shall fight in the fields and in the streets, we shall fight in the hills; we shall never surrender.

WINSTON CHURCHILL
Speech in the House of Commons on 18th June 1940

What General Weygand called the Battle of France is over. I expect that the battle of Britain is about to begin. Upon this battle depends the survival of Christian civilisation. Upon it depends our own British life, and the long continuity of our institutions and our Empire. The whole fury and might of the enemy must very soon be turned on us. Hitler knows that he will have to break us in this island or lose the war. If we can stand up to him, all Europe may be free and the life of the world may move forward into broad, sunlit uplands. But if we fail, then the whole world, including the United States, including all that we have known and cared for, will sink into the abyss of a new dark age made more sinister, and perhaps more protracted, by the lights of perverted science. Let us therefore brace ourselves to our duties, and so bear ourselves that, if the British Empire and its Commonwealth last for a thousand years, men will still say, 'This was their finest hour'.

Though the war ended in 1945, compulsory National Service was to put men into uniform until 1960.

SONGS

THE 23RD PSALM
THE KING JAMES BIBLE

THE LORD IS MY shepherd: I shall not want.

He maketh me to lie down in green pastures: he leadeth me beside the still waters.

He restoreth my soul: He leadeth me in the paths of righteousness for his name's sake.

Yea, though I walk through the valley of the shadow of death, I will fear no evil: for thou art with me; thy rod and thy staff they comfort me.

Thou preparest a table before me in the presence of mine enemies: Thou anointest my head with oil; my cup runneth over.

Surely goodness and mercy shall follow me all the days of my life: and I will dwell in the house of the Lord for ever.

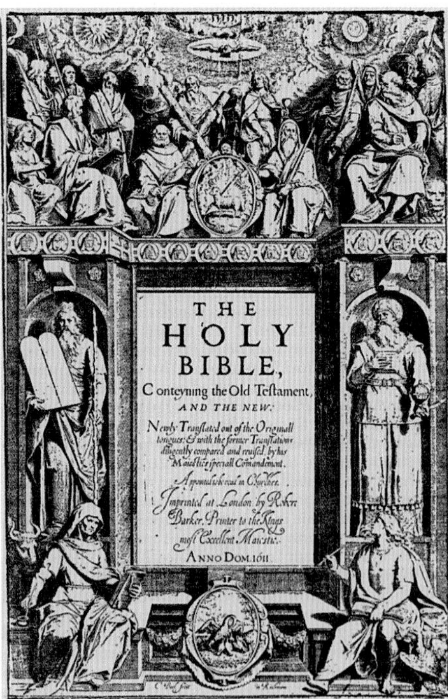

'GOD SAVE THE KING' (1745)
WORDS ATTRIBUTED TO HENRY CAREY (1687–1743)
MUSIC BY DR THOMAS ARNE (1710–78)

GOD SAVE OUR gracious King;
Long live our noble King;
God save the King!
Send him victorious,
Happy and glorious,
Long to reign over us
God save the King!

O Lord our God arise,
Scatter his enemies,
And make them fall:
Confound their politics,
Frustrate their knavish tricks,
On Thee our hopes we fix;
God save us all!

Thy choicest gifts in store
On him be pleased to pour;
Long may he reign:
May he defend our laws,
And ever give us cause
To sing with heart and voice,
God save the King!

The original title page of the Authorised Bible of 1611.

'RULE, BRITANNIA!' (1740)

Words by James Thompson (1700–48)
Music by Dr Thomas Arne (1710–78)

When Britain first, at Heaven's command,
Arose from out the azure main,
This was the charter of the land,
And guardian angels sang this strain –
'Rule, Britannia! Britannia, rule the waves;
Britons never, never, never shall be slaves.'

The nations, not so blest as thee,
Must in their turns to tyrants fall,
Whilst thou shalt flourish great and free,
The dread and envy of them all.
Rule, Britannia! etc.

Still more majestic shalt thou rise,
More dreadful from each foreign stroke,
As the loud blast that tears the skies,
Serves but to root thy native oak.
Rule, Britannia! etc.

Thee haughty tyrants ne'er shall tame,
All their attempts to bend thee down,
Will but arouse thy generous flame,
And work their woe and thy renown.
Rule, Britannia! etc.

To thee belongs the rural reign,
Thy cities shall with commerce shine,
And thine shall be the subject main,
And every shore it circles thine.
Rule, Britannia! etc.

The Muses, still with freedom found,
Shall to thy happy coast repair,
Blest isle with matchless beauty crowned,
And manly hearts to guard the fair.
Rule, Britannia! etc.

'JERUSALEM' (1915)

Words by William Blake (1757–1827)
Music by Hubert Parry (1848–1918)

And did those feet in ancient times,
Walk upon England's mountains green?
And was the holy Lamb of God,
On England's pleasant pastures seen?
And did the countenance divine,
Shine forth upon our clouded hills?
And was Jerusalem builded here,
Among these dark Satanic mills?

Bring me my bow of burning gold!
Bring me my arrows of desire!
Bring me my spear! O clouds unfold!
Bring me my chariot of fire!
I will not cease from mental fight,
Nor shall my sword sleep in my hand,
Till we have built Jerusalem,
In England's green and pleasant land.

'I VOW TO THEE MY COUNTRY' (1918)

WORDS BY CECIL SPRING-RICE (1859–1918)
MUSIC BY GUSTAV HOLST (1874–1934)

I VOW TO THEE, my country all earthly things above,
Entire and whole and perfect, the service of my love;
The love that asks no question, the love that stands the test,
That lays upon the altar the dearest and the best;
The love that never falters, the love that pays the price,
The love that makes undaunted the final sacrifice.

And there's another country, I've heard of long ago,
Most dear to them that love her, most great to them that know;
We may not count her armies, we may not see her King,
Her fortress is a faithful heart, her pride is suffering;
And soul by soul and silently her shining bounds increase,
And her ways are ways of gentleness and all her paths are peace.

'LAND OF HOPE AND GLORY' (1897)

WORDS BY ARTHUR C. BENSON (1862–1925)
MUSIC BY EDWARD ELGAR (1857–1934)

DEAR LAND OF HOPE, thy hope is crowned.
God make thee mightier yet!
On Sov'ran brows, beloved, renowned,
Once more thy crown is set.
Thine equal laws, by Freedom gained,
Have ruled thee well and long;
By Freedom gained, by Truth maintained,
Thine Empire shall be strong.

Chorus
Land of Hope and Glory,
Mother of the Free,
How shall we extol thee,
Who are born of thee?
Wider still and wider
Shall thy bounds be set;
God, who made thee mighty,
Make thee mightier yet.

Thy fame is ancient as the days,
As Ocean large and wide:
A pride that dares and heeds not praise,
A stern and silent pride:
Not that false joy that dreams content
With what our sires have won;
The blood a hero sire hath spent
Still nerves a hero son.

Chorus

THE BRITISH EMPIRE AND IMPERIAL TERRITORIES IN 1920 AND THE YEAR IN WHICH THEY CAME UNDER BRITISH CONTROL

Aden 1839
Alberta *c.* 1788
Anglo-Egyptian Sudan 1899
Antigua 1632
Bahamas 1666
Barbados 1605
Basutoland 1868
Bechuanaland Protectorate 1885
Bengal 1633
Bermudas 1609
Bhutan 1864
Bombay 1608
British Columbia 1821
British Honduras 1638
British North Borneo 1881
British Somaliland 1884
Brunei 1888
Burma 1824
Cameroon 1919
Cape Breton Island 1758
Cape of Good Hope (Cape Colony) 1795
Cayman Islands 1670
Ceylon 1795
Cyprus 1878
Demerara, Berbice, Essequibo 1796
Dominica 1761
Eastern Bengal & Assam 1825
Egypt 1882
Falkland Islands 1765
Federated Malay States 1874
Gambia *c.* 1618
Gibraltar 1704
Gold Coast Colony *c.* 1650
Grenada 1762
Hong Kong 1841
Iraq 1920
Jamaica 1655
Kenya Colony 1888
Lagos 1861
Madras 1639
Malta 1800
Manitoba 1811
Mauritius 1810
Montserrat 1632
Natal 1824
Nevis 1628
New Brunswick 1713
New South Wales 1788
New Zealand 1840
Newfoundland 1583
Nigeria 1884
Nova Scotia 1623
Nyasaland Protectorate 1891
Ontario 1759
Orange River Colony 1848
Palestine 1919
Prince Edward Island 1758
Punjab 1849
Quebec 1759
Queensland 1824
Rhodesia 1888
Rupert's Land and North-West Territory 1670
St Christopher (St Kitts) 1623
St Lucia 1605
St Vincent 1762
Sarawak 1888
Saskatchewan 1766
Seychelles 1794
Sierra Leone 1787
Singapore 1819
South Australia 1836
South West Africa 1919
Straits Settlements 1786
Swaziland 1890
Tanganyika Territory 1919
Tasmania 1803
Tobago 1763
Togoland 1919
Transjordan 1920
Transvaal 1877
Trinidad 1797
Uganda 1890
Vancouver Island 1821
Victoria 1834
Virgin Islands 1666
Western Australia 1826
Zanzibar Protectorate 1890
Zululand 1887

IMPERIAL WEIGHTS AND MEASURES

c. 1830

Length

1 mile = 1,760 yards
1 furlong = 220 yards
1 chain = 22 yards = 100 links
1 rod, pole or perch = 5½ yards
1 yard = 3 feet = 36 inches
1 foot = 12 inches
1 span = 9 inches
1 hand = 4 inches
1 nail = 2¼ inches (for cloth)
1 inch = 1/36th of a yard
1 fathom = 6 feet
1 cable = 600 feet
1 nautical mile = 6,080 feet

Liquid volume (beer and ale)

1 tun = 2 butts
1 butt = 2 hogsheads
1 hogshead = 1½ barrels
1 barrel = 2 kilderkins
1 kilderkin = 2 firkins
1 firkin = 9 gallons
1 gallon = 4 quarts
1 quart = 2 pints
1 pint = 4 gills
1 gill = 5 fluid ounces
1 fluid ounce = 8 fluid drachms
1 fluid drachm = 60 minims

Area

1 square mile = 640 acres
1 acre = 10 sq chains = 4 roods
1 rood = 40 sq poles
1 sq pole = 30¼ sq yards
1 sq yard = 9 sq feet
1 sq foot = 144 sq inches

Dry measure

1 chaldron = 36 bushels
1 quarter = 8 bushels
1 bushel = 4 pecks
1 peck = 2 gallons
1 gallon = 4 quarts
1 quart = 2 pints
1 pint = 4 gills

Money

1 guinea = 21 shillings
1 pound sterling = 20 shillings
1 crown = 5 shillings
1 shilling = 12 pence
1 penny = 4 farthings

Weight avoirdupois

1 ton = 20 hundredweight (cwt)
1 hundredweight = 4 quarters
1 quarter = 2 stones
1 stone = 14 pounds (lb)
1 pound = 16 ounces (oz) = 7,000 grains
1 ounce = 16 drams = 437½ grains
1 dram = 27.34 grains

BRITISH MILITARY AND CIVILIAN HONOURS

THE VICTORIA CROSS (VC)

The highest military award for conspicuous bravery in the presence of the enemy

Instituted by Queen Victoria in 1856, the VC consists of a bronze Maltese cross and the royal crown, with a lion in the centre, under which are the words 'For Valour'. The ribbon is claret-coloured. Worn on the left breast, it takes precedence over all other decorations.

Until 1942, the VC was manufactured from the metal of guns captured in the Crimean War at Sebastopol. To date, 1,355 have been awarded.

THE GEORGE CROSS (GC)

The highest civilian award 'for acts of the greatest heroism or of the most conspicuous courage in circumstances of extreme danger', the GC is only awarded to service personnel for acts of heroism not covered by military honours.

Instituted in 1940, the GC consists of a silver cross with St George and the Dragon in the centre. The words 'For Gallantry' encircle St George and the Dragon. It hangs from a dark blue ribbon.

The GC has been awarded to 156 people, 84 posthumously. The island of Malta in 1942, and the Royal Ulster Constabulary in 1999 were awarded the decoration collectively.

THE MOST NOBLE ORDER OF THE GARTER (KG)

The highest order of the Knighthood in Great Britain, the KG was instituted by King Edward III in 1348, when the Countess of Salisbury lost her garter dancing at a court ball. On noticing the knowing looks as he picked it up, King Edward tied the blue garter round his own knee saying 'Honi soit qui mal y pense' (shame on him, who thinks evil), the motto of the order.

Knights of the Garter are chosen personally by the Sovereign as a mark of royal favour and in honour of their contributions to Britain or the Crown. The order is limited to 24 Knights plus Royal Knights. Women became eligible in 1987. Foreign monarchs in the order are known as Stranger Knights and currently include the Emperor of Japan and the Kings of Sweden and Spain. The patron saint of the order is St George.

THE MOST ANCIENT AND MOST NOBLE ORDER OF THE THISTLE (KT)

The second highest order of the Knighthood in Great Britain, founded, according to legend, by King Achaius of the Scots in 787. In its current form it was instituted by James II (VII of Scotland), but fell into abeyance after 1688. It was revived by Queen Anne in 1703. Other than Royal Knights, the KT consists of 16 Knights. It is sometimes called the Order of St Andrew. Women became eligible in 1987.

THE ILLUSTRIOUS ORDER OF ST PATRICK (KP)

Instituted by George III in 1783, the order originally consisted of the Sovereign, the Lord Lieutenant and 15 Knights. In 1833, the number of Knights was enlarged to 22. With the establishment of the Irish Free State in 1922, the order effectively went into abeyance. There have been no elections since 1924. The last surviving recipient, Prince Henry, Duke of Gloucester, died in 1974.

THE MOST HONOURABLE ORDER OF THE BATH

Established by King Henry IV, the Order of the Bath takes its name from the symbolic washing or purification, which originally formed part of a squire's preparations for being knighted, which would also have involved fasting, vigils and prayer. The last time knights were created in the ancient manner was at the coronation of Charles II in 1661.

The order was reinvigorated by George I in 1725. It consisted of the Sovereign, a Great Master and 36 Knights:

'Whereas in a case of a war in Europe we are determined that this Realm should be in a posture of defence against the attempts of our enemies We do hereby ordain that from henceforth every Companion of the said Military Order in case of any danger of invasion from foreign enemies or from rebellion at home shall maintain at his own cost four men-at-arms for any number of days the Sovereign shall think proper.'

After the Battle of Waterloo the order was split into two divisions, military and civil, and expanded. The ancient rites of bathing and fasting were abolished. The motto of the order is 'Tria juncto in uno' (Three joined in one), the 'three' being England, Scotland and France and the Holy Trinity. Women were first admitted in 1971. The order is principally awarded to members of the armed forces.

The order now consists of the Sovereign, Great Master and three classes of members:

120 Knights or Dames Grand Cross (KGCB)

295 Knights or Dames Commander (KCB)

1,455 companions (not knights) (CB)

THE ORDER OF MERIT (OM)

Edward VII created the Order of Merit in 1902, the first British Order to admit men and women on equal terms, limited to 24 members, but not conferring any title. It is often awarded for services to the sciences and the arts.

BARONET

In order to raise money for the defence of the Plantation of Ulster, James I instituted the hereditary title of baronet in 1611. The title was effectively sold in exchange for 'funds'. The Red Hand of Ulster became the badge of baronets of England, Great Britain, the United Kingdom and Ireland; and of Scotland and Nova Scotia in 1625.

BANNERET

Last properly conferred by Charles I in 1642 on Colonel John Smith for his recapture of the Royal Standard at the battle of Edgehill, this order of Knighthood was conferred on the field of battle for acts of exceptional gallantry by tearing off the points of the recipient's pennant (the banner under which the captain had lead his vassals into battle).

THE MOST EXALTED ORDER OF THE STAR OF INDIA

Instituted in 1861 by Queen Victoria, membership of the Order was awarded for services to the Indian Empire. There were three classes:

Knight Grand Commander (rather than Knight Grand Cross, since the cross of Christianity might offend inhabitants of the predominantly non-Christian India) in the Most Exalted Order of the Star of India (GCSI)

Knight Commander in the Most Exalted Order of the Star of India (KCSI)

Companion in the Most Exalted Order of the Star of India (CSI)
The order was discontinued in 1947.

THE MOST DISTINGUISHED ORDER OF ST MICHAEL AND ST GEORGE

Instituted in 1818 to commemorate the Ionian Islands coming under British protection, the order was initially conferred upon those with important responsibilities in the Mediterranean. The order was soon extended to those who had given distinguished service in foreign affairs generally and especially those who render extraordinary service in a foreign country, or in relation to the British Dominions, Colonies or Commonwealth.

The order consists of the Sovereign, Grand Master and three classes:

125 Knights and Dames Grand Cross (GCMG) [God calls me God]

375 Knights and Dames Commander (KCMG) [Kindly call me God]

1,375 Companions (CMG) [Call me God]

The order's motto is 'Auspicium melioras aevi' (Token of a better age).

THE MOST EMINENT ORDER OF THE INDIAN EMPIRE

Instituted in 1877 for services to India, the order includes three classes:

Knight Grand Commander in the Most Eminent Order of the Indian Empire (GCIE)

Knight Commander in the Most Eminent Order of the Indian Empire (KCIE)

Companion in the Most Eminent Order of the Indian Empire (CIE)

THE ORDER OF THE CROWN OF INDIA (CI)

Queen Victoria created two exclusively female orders, the Order of the Crown of India and the Royal Order of Victoria and Albert. Both are now defunct.

THE ROYAL VICTORIAN ORDER

Instituted by Queen Victoria in 1896, the order is entirely within the Sovereign's personal gift, rather than by ministerial recommendation.

The order consists of five classes:

Knights Grand Cross in the Royal Victorian Order (GCVO)

Knights Commander in the Royal Victorian Order (KCVO)

Commander in the Royal Victorian Order (CVO)

Lieutenant in the Royal Victorian Order (LVO)

Member in the Royal Victorian Order (MVO)

ORDER OF THE BRITISH EMPIRE

INSTITUTED BY George V in 1917, the award honours those who have rendered service to the United Kingdom and its people and is split into Military and Civil Divisions. There are now over 100,000 living members of the order in Britain and abroad. From its very inception the order included women and foreigners who had contributed to the British war effort. The motto of the order is 'For God and the Empire'.

The order consists of five classes:

Knights (or Dames) Grand Cross in the Most Excellent Order of the British Empire (GBE)

Knights (or Dames) in the Most Excellent Order of the British Empire (KBE)

Commander in the Most Excellent Order of the British Empire (CBE)

Officer in the Most Excellent Order of the British Empire (OBE)

Member in the Most Excellent Order of the British Empire (MBE)

ORDER OF THE COMPANIONS OF HONOUR

INSTITUTED IN 1917 by George V, the order is conferred on men and women for services of national importance. The order consists of the Sovereign and 65 ordinary members. The motto of the order is 'In action faithful and in honour clear'.

DISTINGUISHED SERVICE ORDER (DSO)

INSTITUTED BY Queen Victoria in 1886, the order is awarded for meritorious or distinguished services by members of the armed forces of the rank of major (or its equivalent), or above during wartime. (The DSO is very rarely awarded to especially gallant more junior officers.)

'Gold cross, enamelled white, edged gold, having on one side thereof in the centre, within a wreath of laurel enamelled green, the Imperial Crown in gold upon a red enamelled ground and on the reverse, within a similar wreath on a similar red ground, Our Imperial and Royal cypher, VRI, shall be suspended from the left breast by a red riband, edged blue, of one inch in width.'

CONSPICUOUS GALLANTRY CROSS (CGC)

INSTITUTED IN 1995 by Queen Elizabeth II, the CGC is awarded for conspicuous gallantry in action, performed by all ranks of the armed services. The ribbon is white with a red central stripe and blue edges.

DISTINGUISHED SERVICE CROSS (DSC)

INSTITUTED BY King Edward VII in 1901 (as the Conspicuous Service Cross), the DSC is awarded for gallant or distinguished naval service in the face of the enemy. The ribbon is blue with a white central stripe.

MILITARY CROSS (MC)

INSTITUTED BY King George V in 1914, the MC is awarded for gallant and distinguished services in action. The ribbon is white with a purple central stripe.

DISTINGUISHED FLYING CROSS (DFC)

INSTITUTED BY King George V in 1918, the DFC is awarded for courage or devotion to duty while flying in active service against the enemy. The ribbon is white with diagonal purple stripes.

AIR FORCE CROSS (AFC)

INSTITUTED BY King George V in 1918, the AFC is awarded for courage or devotion to duty while flying. The ribbon is white with diagonal red stripes.

DISTINGUISHED CONDUCT MEDAL (DCM)

INSTITUTED IN 1854, the DCM is awarded to other ranks for acts of gallantry in action. The ribbon is red with a dark blue central stripe.

CONSPICUOUS GALLANTRY MEDAL (CGM)

INSTITUTED IN 1855 (for the Crimean War only), and reinstituted in 1874, it was replaced by the Conspicuous Gallantry Cross in 1993. The CGM is awarded to other ranks in the Royal Navy, Royal Marines or merchant navy for acts of gallantry in action. The ribbon is white with dark blue edges.

THE GEORGE MEDAL (GM)

INSTITUTED IN 1940, the GM is awarded for outstanding acts of bravery that nevertheless do not qualify for the George Cross. A round medal, with St George and the Dragon on one side and the head of the monarch on the reverse, it hangs from a red ribbon with five narrow blue stripes.

DISTINGUISHED SERVICE MEDAL (DSM)

INSTITUTED IN 1914, the DSM is awarded to other ranks of the Royal Navy or Royal Marines for distinguished conduct in the face of the enemy. The ribbon is blue with a double white central stripe.

MILITARY MEDAL (MM)

INSTITUTED IN 1916, the MM is awarded to other ranks of the army and Royal Air Force for acts of bravery in the field. The blue ribbon has a white central stripe bearing two red stripes.

DISTINGUISHED FLYING MEDAL (DFM)

INSTITUTED IN 1918, the DFM is awarded to other ranks of the Royal Air Force for acts of bravery while flying in the face of the enemy. The ribbon is white with narrow diagonal purple stripes.

AIR FORCE MEDAL (AFM)

AWARDED TO other ranks of the Royal Air Force for courage or devotion to duty in the air. The ribbon is white with narrow diagonal red stripes.

MENTION IN DESPATCHES

CURRENT BRITISH DEPENDENCIES

Anguilla
Ascension Island
Bermuda
The British Antarctic Territory
The British Indian Ocean Territory
The British Virgin Islands
The Cayman Islands
The Channel Islands
The Falkland Islands

FALKLAND ISLANDS

TURKS & CAICOS ISLANDS

ISLE OF MAN

JERSEY

Gibraltar
The Isle of Man
Montserrat
Pitcairn Island
The South Georgia and the South Sandwich Islands
The Turks and Caicos Islands
St Helena

CURRENT MEMBERS OF THE COMMONWEALTH

Antigua & Barbuda
Australia
The Bahamas
Bangladesh
Barbados
Belize
Botswana
Brunei
Cameroon
Canada
Cyprus
Dominica
Fiji *(left 1987, rejoined 1997, suspended 2000, readmitted 2001)*
The Gambia
Ghana
Grenada
Guyana
India
Jamaica
Kenya
Kiribati
Lesotho
Malawi
Malaysia
The Maldives
Malta
Mauritius
Mozambique
Namibia
Nauru
New Zealand
Nigeria *(suspended 1995, rejoined 1999)*
Pakistan *(left 1972, rejoined 1989)*
Papua New Guinea
St Kitts & Nevis
St Lucia
St Vincent & the Grenadines
Samoa
The Seychelles
Sierra Leone
Singapore
The Solomon Islands
South Africa *(left 1961, rejoined 1994)*
Sri Lanka
Swaziland
Tanzania *(Tanganyika & Zanzibar jointly formed Tanzania in 1964)*
Tonga
Trinidad & Tobago
Tuvalu
Uganda
The United Kingdom
Vanuatu
Zambia

The Irish Free State and Zimbabwe have left the Commonwealth.

CANADA

AUSTRALIA

NEW ZEALAND

SOUTH AFRICA

JURY SERVICE

Persons eligible for Jury Service include:

- Any person registered as a parliamentary or local government elector between the ages of 18 and 70 who has been resident in the United Kingdom, Channel Islands or Isle of Man for at least five years, since the age of 13

Persons ineligible for Jury Service:

- The judiciary, including judges
- Those involved in the administration of justice, including barristers, solicitors, forensic scientists, prison governors and policemen
- The clergy, including men in holy orders; regular ministers of any religious denomination; and vowed members of religious orders
- The mentally ill

Persons disqualified from Jury Service:

- Any person sentenced to more than five years in prison
- Any person who has served any part of a sentence of imprisonment during the previous ten years
- Any person who has been placed on probation during the last five years
- Any person on bail

Historically, the British have enjoyed absolute equality before the law. Juries are not accountable to the State. Defendants are innocent until proven guilty.

Persons excused from Jury Service:

- Persons over 65
- Members and Officers of the Houses of Parliament and of the Scottish Parliament
- European MPs
- Welsh and Northern Irish Assembly members
- Serving members of HM naval, air, or military forces
- Registered, practising doctors, dentists, nurses, midwives, vets and pharmacists
- Those practising members of religious orders whose beliefs are incompatible with jury service
- Any person who has previously served on a jury within two years of a summons

THE UNION FLAG

THE FLAG OF THE UNITED KINGDOM OF GREAT BRITAIN AND NORTHERN IRELAND

KING JAMES I of England (VI of Scotland) introduced the Union Flag in 1606. He signed the proclamation with the French version of his name, 'Jacques', as his mother, Mary Queen of Scots and one-time Queen of France, had written it; hence the Union Jacques or Jack.

Though commonly called the Union Jack, its official name is the Union Flag, and it is only formally described as the Union Jack when flying from the Jack Staff of a British ship of war. Unlike the flags of all other nations, the Union is not, in fact, a national flag. It is a royal flag which theoretically only the Sovereign or her representatives are entitled to use. By long established custom, this means in practice that every British subject may fly the flag on land, as confirmed in parliament in 1908 and again in 1933; but when on water the Red Ensign, the Cross of St George, the Cross of St Andrew or the Welsh Dragon should be used instead.

The Union Flag consists of the flags of three saints: St George, St Andrew and St Patrick. Because of the way in which the heralds have offset St Patrick's saltire, the Union Flag is not symmetrical.

The Union Flag should normally be flown with the Cross of St Andrew taking precedence as the older flag, above that of St Patrick (which was added in 1801 when the Act of Union created the United Kingdom of Great Britain and Ireland); with the broad white diagonal on top next to the pole. If flown the other way up, it becomes a signal of distress.

THE UNION FLAG IS FLOWN OFFICIALLY AT THE OPENING AND PROROGATION OF PARLIAMENT AND ALSO ON THE FOLLOWING DAYS:

The Queen's Accession	6th February
Prince Andrew's Birthday	19th February
St David's Day (Wales)	1st March
Prince Edward's Birthday	10th March
Commonwealth Day	2nd Monday in March
The Queen's Birthday	21st April
St George's Day (England)	23rd April
Europe Day	9th May
Coronation Day	2nd June
The Duke of Edinburgh's Birthday	10th June
The Queen's Official Birthday	June (varies)
Princess Anne's Birthday	15th August
Remembrance Sunday	November (varies)
The Prince of Wales' Birthday	14th November
The Queen's Wedding Anniversary	20th November
St Andrew's Day	30th November

THE TECHNICAL DESCRIPTION OF THE UNION FLAG BY ORDER OF COUNCIL:

'The Union Flag shall be azure, the Crosses saltire of St Andrew and St Patrick quarterly per saltire, counter-changed, argent and gules, the latter fimbriated of the second, surmounted by the Cross of St. George of the third fimbriated as the saltire.'

THE ARTICLES OF THE ACT OF UNION, 1707

I That the two kingdoms of England and Scotland shall for ever after be united into one kingdom by the name of Great Britain.
II That the succession to the monarchy of the united kingdom of Great Britain be to the most excellent Princess Sophia of Hanover, and the heirs of her body being Protestants.
III That the united kingdom of Great Britain be represented by one Parliament.
IV That all the subjects of the united kingdom of Great Britain shall have full freedom to trade within the said united kingdom.
V That all ships belonging to her Majesty's subjects of Scotland be deemed as ships of Great Britain.
VI That all parts of the united kingdom shall have the same allowances and be under the same prohibitions and regulations of trade and liable to the same Customs and duties on import and export.
VII That all parts of the united kingdom be liable to the same Excise upon all excisable liquors.
VIII That all foreign salt imported into Scotland shall be charged the same duties as [in] England. But Scotland shall, for seven years, be exempted from paying [the duty] in Scotland for salt made there.
IX That Scotland shall not be charged the sum of forty-eight thousand pounds as the quota of Scotland to a land tax.
X That Scotland shall not be charged with the same duties on stamped paper, vellum and parchment in force in England.
XI That Scotland shall not be charged with the duties payable in England on windows and lights.
XII That Scotland shall not be charged with the duties payable in England on coals, culm and cinders not consumed in Scotland.
XIII That Scotland shall not be charged with the duty payable in England upon malt.
XIV That Scotland shall not be charged with any other duties except these consented to in this treaty.
XV It is agreed that Scotland shall have an equivalent for what [her] subjects shall be charged towards payment of the debts of England . . . the sum of three hundred ninety-eight thousand and eighty-five pounds ten shillings.
XVI That the coin shall be the same standard and value throughout the united kingdom.

INDEX

ACKNOWLEDGEMENTS

Without the tireless support and enthusiasm of my darling wife Fiona this book would never have reached the bookshelves. I thank her and my three sons, George, Hamish and Augustine, with all my heart.

I also owe an enormous debt of gratitude to my old school friend Giles Morland for his total conviction from the outset and instant offer of financial backing; to Nick May and everyone at Cameron May for their exhaustive technical, administrative and moral support; to Tony Duckworth for his patience and generosity; to my parents, brother and sisters, especially Henrietta; to my headhunting colleagues, especially Rupert White and Benedict Fenwick, and to all the friends who read the manuscript before publication, especially Simon Leary.

Almost single-handedly Robert Hardman was responsible for generating the initial media interest and I thank John Saumarez Smith of Heywood Hill and Graham Greene of John Sandoe, originally the only two booksellers willing to stock any copies.

My thanks also to John Beveridge, Robin Birley, Dermot Chichester, Charles Clover, James Edgedale, Nick Georgiou, Greville Howard, Dan Jacobs, Andrew Roberts, Adrian Sykes, Andrew Yates, and, of course, Carey Smith, Natalie Hunt and Caroline Newbury at Ebury Press.

Finally I would like to thank all the readers of *The Pocket Book of Patriotism* who wrote sending good wishes and suggestions, many of which have been included in this expanded, illustrated edition.